GUNS

<u>GUNS</u>

GUNS

Researched by and writings of Appleton Schneider

ISBN 5800109831896

Regarding guns, shootings, schools, etc.

It seems the Connecticut shooting is epic tragedy, catastrophe, atrocity. Little kids mowed down. Twenty, I believe. The internet coverage showed a little girl's portrait, her beautiful innocence and joy to be alive vividly embodied. Eyes sparkling toward the camera that took her . . . maybe last . . . picture.
My eyes are tear-filled even now, remembering. The tears ranneth over back then when I wrote this.
It seems quite unlikely that anyone, in individual acts (not militia or military) would commit such carnage with any other sort of weapon than a gun. "Students armed with hunting knives rampaged through the corridors and classrooms of the school, stabbing and slicing . . . ." ?? Yes, it could happen. But, and has happened since the Connecticut incident. But massacres with other than guns, such as knives, are far less likely. Forcible deterrence by others would likely subdue the attacker(s) prior to multi-massacre. And, preemptively, so to speak, the requirement of "touch") another human (to stab the victim) would provide at least some degree of reticence. To pull a trigger from a distance takes place in a context that places shooter and shootee(s) as if conceptually apart from "fellow-humans" status.

But those who maim and kill don't confine their acts within such "humanistic-abstractions".

If guns could be removed from existence, that would solve the gun problem. But it wouldn't provide anyone with any protection from the intentions and inflictions of evil (from robbery to rape to massacre) of those individuals who would still exist as criminal or deranged.

Making possession of guns a crime of commission -- would be committing a crime of omission by depriving people (and in really bad socio-scenarios a populace) of the means to protect and even preserve themselves.

For, yes, it's not guns per se that are killers. It's killers using guns.

If extreme gun control could be legislated, enacted, enforced (as should be the case), it still wouldn't solve the problem of guns in the wrong hands -- or being fired by those hands into theaters of people or classrooms of students. But at least there'd be some semblance of the same sort of "screening" process -- required for one to get a driver's license, an insurance policy, a job, etc. etc. One's "record" should have to be checked before he's provided the "vehicle" to . . . drive a bullet. Background check. No over-the-counter sales anywhere. Gun shows included.

Gun-purchase and ownership even by Constitutional "de-amendment" (of Constitutional amendment) would be little more effective than Prohibition was in keeping alcohol and all its deleterious effects away from the people. A "war on weapons" would be as effective as our ongoing "war on drugs". Or that foregoing war on alcoholic beverages.

For no matter what, those who want to obtain whatever kind of gun will somehow get ahold of them. Through the black market. By means of the "leakage" (or distribution) from weapons-dealing of obsolete or excess military (per se) stockpiles. Even the actually illegal-to-possess military machine gun genre are somewhere out there on the private market, perhaps having passed through some African warlord nation on the way to the US urban realm.

No matter what we do, we can no more successfully disarm the people than we can dis-booze them!! Or de-drug those who want to use drugs.

Guns are part of existence, And any actual comparison of gun ownership to drugs or booze is really irrational

Guns ownership is actually increasing, "right-to-carry" (even"-concealed") being legislated here and there. People are providing themselves with protection from what can't be removed as potential threat even to life and limb, theirs and their children's.

And there does seem logic in this "municipal militia" mentality. Only a totally psycho shooter is not going to give some thought to commencing fire where he knows that in quick response someone else's gun is going to cease his firing as he drops wounded or dead.

But there's a problem with a totally armed populace. The incidences of shootings that occur due to drunken disputes or marital-manics or mall-security-mentality-armed neighborhood watchmen . . . . also "accidental" or "lost-control" shootings . . . . keep showing up in the papers and online.

Simply, so far,
Making gun possession illegal is to make the populace vulnerable not only to criminals, but to possible insurrectionists, jihadists, etc. (Consider the differential outcome aloft on 9/11 had at least a few of the passengers been armed!!! . . . . . or in Connecticut most recently had there been someone to shoot down the shooter).

The increase in gun ownership, "right-to-carry" rules, etc. is indicative not of just some "popular" trend -- but of the recognition of a need, if not necessity, by a population. What if, in the middle of the night, someone was breaking down your door or already in your bedroom with bad intentions? You don't have a weapon? You're screwed, perhaps, depending, more than one way. At the other extreme of example, consider how different might have been Germany's rail transport volume had the Jewish population been armed!!

The Constitution aside (" . . right to 'bear arms' . . "), granting the right to weapon ownership by "the people", any attempt to remove guns from the people would be as counter-productive as Prohibition. The "problem" situation would not only persist under cover, but proliferate to encompass absolute illegality rather than accepted and appropriate manufacturers and markets of a profitable product.

And using guns for recreation, hobby, hunting, skill . . . . that's what the millions of gun owners do with their guns. The fraction of gun wielders that kill, especially catastrophically, is almost insignificant (statistically, of course, not in the sense of the grief and outrage that results from their having . . . mental problems.

There should be another consideration to just what carnage committed by guns represents . . . statistically. For example, what are the actual probabilities that in any day's duration a kid is going to be injured or killed in an auto? As a pedestrian? In a sport (such as, especially, hockey or football resulting even in paralysis in the short term, for football brain damage as eventuality). Would we find that other factors present higher odds that a child (or anyone) will be a victim . . . than of a gun?

For all the kids that get creamed in cars or on bikes, there's no clamor to get those devices out of the hands of people. Now and again (I'd venture at least as frequently as we hear of mass-shootings in schools) there's a school bus overturning or submerging and multiple young lives lost or severely damaged). Should we ban school buses? School bus drivers?

Of course the horror, the anguish (even vicarious, the response of one who doesn't even know any of those Conn. kids or their families), the actual sense of bereavement. . is a necessary primacy of expression. Humanity sharing its "kinship even of "unrelatedness".

But beyond the outrage and outreach (even within ourselves -- as if our souls to touch with those of the actual victims) . . . beyond that "emotional" dimension, we need to think. Rationally. What possibility can be implemented to intercept the next intention of carnage. But what probability is the "tragedy" but an "excruciating extravaganza" event within ongoing injury and dying and disabling inflicted by so many aspects of life. Other than guns. Far more frequent (some constant, every day) than gun deaths.

Massacres by guns are in ways proportionate to commercial aircraft crashes. Spectacular. Horrific. Anguishing. But damned infrequent.

So, assuming as I have above, that we're not going to get rid of guns (because we can't and even shouldn't and things are going in the opposite direction anyway with more and more people getting guns). . . . . . .
So, realizing that among those who have guns there will likely be another "killer" (not self-defensor) personality/intention . . . . .
The latest (of a somewhat separated-series of shootings) -- the Conn. school: What can we do to protect the kids?
One suggestion has been to place an armed guard in every school.
Already sports and arts and performance programs are being terminated due to insufficient funding. Kids are having to bring in their own paper and pencils -- or teachers purchasing supplies out of their meager earnings.
So who'll pay for the guard?
Okay, say there's a volunteer guard corps so guards are affordable. In comes the shooter who's cased the place and recognized the guard (not difficult to differentiate from a teacher, or especially from being a student). Shooter shoots in an area where the guard isn't!! (Quite a different situational context, a school building with armed guard -- from a commercial airplane containing same)
Or, more "logically", the shooter just shoots the guard before proceeding with the academic personnel in the place.

More sensibly, teachers should be armed.
With school budgets so distressed, they'd have to pay for the pistols themselves out of their meager salaries. Perhaps the type of weapon would be designated.
Oh, but what if one of the teachers flipped-out and commenced killing as a last-resort attempt to exercise some kind of classroom control?
But at least armed school personnel would distribute deterrence as well as possibly preemptive firing upon a shooter -- or take him down quickly.
As for arming all the kids? The gun-making lobby and NRA would likely be in favor. No more toy guns. Who needs 'em? Real ones!! Each kid a self-sufficient savior, perhaps of his classmates (and , , hmmm . . the teacher too . . .or not) and himself by being able to shoot down a shooter who's come into the building. With intensive instruction and training, even a young child should be a responsible gun-owner and handler. Look back to the frontier days for the actual adult potential that even young kids can enact.

Oh, but there's the problem that we've seen rather often in the inner-city neighborhoods and even school yards where kids have guns and it just escalates shootings.
Even in contexts that reveal killer-mentality as psychosis (but a "group-mindset" actually espoused by "gang" or "hood" or even "latent tribal-heritage".
The most horrific such case I've run across involved an early grade-school kid in the school playground. Behind him was a little girl classmate. He noticed, pulled out the pistol, and point blank shot her through the head.

Interrogated . . . ."Why . . . ."
"She dissed me!!"
"She 'dissed' you?"
"Tha' wha' ah say. She dissed me bad."
"How'd she 'diss' you?"
And the kid replied with pride in his prowess, priority . . .
"SHE STEP ON MAH SHADOW !!!"

We'd better make gun ownership subject to perhaps the same age-determinations as driver's licenses -- and require that one study a handbook and take a test including "driving" (firing) guns, maintaining, cleaning, locking, etc. For general purchase there should be a background check via internet data-base. So maybe you have to wait a couple days to go pick up your piece?
There has to be some level of "control", at least by screening, surveillance, registration. (as with, motorcycle, even boat!! -- either of which kill almost exclusively by sheer accident. In very few cases does one "aim the Harley or jet-ski as a killer-projectile). But there can't and shouldn't be any attempt to disarm "the people".
For it can't be done, even if gun possession became capital crime.
There'd still be those with guns.
And they'd be the real bad ones.
Which, at an extreme, would not be isolated loonies,
But organized, even in quasi-governmental
formats such as SS . . . .

And . . . . there are plenty of those out there in every state in this country, intent to take over the country. Anarchist-survivalists are the greater threat to our liberty than any governmental attempt to make gun-ownership a bit comparable to owner- and "operator-ship" of so many things – even Harleys. It would be the insurrectionists who'd take over America, kill off the present representatives and officials, and . . . . take away everyone else's guns but their echelon,

    After Sandy Hook (Conn. Shooting), there was a suggestion made to have military personnel guard schools, even be stationed within.
    The Military should be totally banned from nurseries, and from preschools and kindergartens.
    But seriously, in secondary schools, to include discipline, group (corps included) orientation and dedication (rather than just autonomy) would actually be an addend to learning and experience. A dimension of decorum within formal contexts (such as behavior and dress codes in schools) would not be brain-washing youth to become Rambos revved for rampage. Some exposure to discipline, even "periodic-contained regimentation" would not destroy individuality or supervene sensitivity of those not inherently militaristic-material/men or women.
    The presentation of and preparation in combat-related ways and means per se would not promote warriors -- rather, provide a (so to speak) "worst case scenario breadth of information and even ability for . . . civilian defense". Should

there arise an actual insurgent enemy, in this country the population would
be *pre-victims*, helpless, clueless. (what would you do if in the middle of the night
. . . . or even broad daylight . . . loony or criminal or insurrectionist-survivalist
taking over your local government – and you.)?

The paradigm of globalized financial interdependence seems, to me, a
detente and determinant so that waging actual war would be the equivalent of the
aggressor asserting itself by committing suicide of its country's economy, at least.
But the presence of myriad militaries is also a deterrent in a "stand your ground"
global arena. Actual military membership provides our country's strength, starting
with "appearance" and, of course, materiel inventories.
   We may be about to recognize that the most dangerous adversary we face is
NATURE, not each other. Climate change, desertification, storm intensification,
tsunamis, even mutant-resistance disease strains and resurgences are evident.
The most strategic role of organized, "militarized" men and women may soon
significantly include (if not even focus on) winning in "theaters of devastation"
(such as, most recently, the Philippines and Japan). Recognition of the roles
already played by our military in disaster-relief should be a dimension of "learning
and training" most valuable even in a public classroom . . . . . and recognized by
the teaching military that such should be a significant focus of their curriculum.

Additional considerations of protections from projectiles (such as school-shooters
and others).

The NRA's suggestion to have an armed guard in every school could spur one's
approbation-by-comparison . . . to having an armed guard in a Bank, or jewelry store, or
other venue of value. And there is nothing of greater value than children. It's often
occurred to me that the vehicle which conveys the most valuable "cargo" over the
road isn't an armored Wells Fargo (or other) truck. It's a school bus!!
So if we place armed guards in banks and other settings of threat to their contents,
to have same in a school seems, at first, a logical continuum of concern and protection.
But considering logistical (rather than logical) implications and involvements, the NRA
suggestion is absolutely insufficient protection.
For one thing, what if the single armed guard himself goes psycho? Or takes the
job in order to have an "in" to commit mass child-murder?
What if the one armed guard gets sick or is relieving himself when a psycho enters
the building?
What if the lone armed guard is in comprehensive and concerted surveillance of
this part of the building and the psycho shooter starts shooting in that part?
Considering the sprawling size of so many recently built schools, to adequately
patrol the building would the guard have to be mobilized (at least roller-blades, better
still motorized something or other for greater speed)?

Obviously comparing the protection provided by an armed guard in a bank or a store is not analogous to the layout and situation within a school. Banks and stores consist significantly of one big area. Schools consist of at least linears, if not labyrinths, of corridors interconnecting myriad classrooms and labs and gym and cafeteria and offices and closets and much, much more.

Obviously unoccupied chambers don't need an armed guard's presence. The guard's purpose is to protect personnel from harm. Perhaps we can exempt administrative offices etc. as well, and just focus on protecting children. Adult attrition is tragic, but not in comparison to the agonizing atrocity of killed children.

Obviously, the NRA should have advocated having an armed guard not just in every school -- but in every classroom! Corridors full of kids would be protected as the guard from one class would go on to the next room along with the students. One armed guard per school is almost ludicrous.

If uniformed, yes, there might be some even subliminal level of law-enforcement as safety presence (and even personal orientations and interactions between the cop and the kids creating an ongoing rapport even into their adulthood). But if uniformed, obviously the one cop would be obvious and any perpetrator would know to blast his way into the building and through the little bodies at the other end of the edifice.

If plain-clothed, "anonymous", how easily a psycho could "come to work" even just prior to the actual guard -- thus be in the building and kill "prior to protection procedure and authorized personnel on premise".

Any armed guard in a school, if not ludicrous, is quite inadequate protection.

And what about protecting the kids on the way to or from school? Proportionate to even "ludicrous" protections of the school itself might become the threat to the kids in transit! "Taking out " a bus load involves far less hassle and risk than barging into a building. "Swallowing a yellow capsule" of kids in firepower or fire per se might be the next permutation of creative carnage. Why mess with the "stock room of students" when you can destroy the "containerized shipment", so efficiently packaged, so to speak. (Any actual terrorist would surely agree with

So does this mean than we should stop sending kids to school? Or from? Thus we should stop having schools? Everyone should be home-schooled? That would surely solve the problem of massacres (other than of very large families). Mass-killers just aren't going to set up an itinerary or route through neighborhoods in order to wipe out their requisite multiples of little lives.

But, no, mass-home-schooling isn't going to happen. Thankfully.

So we're back to the schools-protection-problem.

Obviously a contingent or phalanx or regiment or even multiple of armed school guards isn't going to happen. Not unless they'd all just volunteer their time unpaid.

From the standpoint of financial feasibility, arming all the teachers and administration would be more likely. From any standpoint other than financial feasibility, of course a "fire-powered faculty" would never be allowed.

Already there are metal detectors scanning and monitoring the kids (and others) entering some schools. Some prevention of "private" acts of assault or even murder may be accomplished, true. But the massacres of innocents takes place, it seems, as the massacrer mashes his way into the building (school or theater) or, takes out his targets in one-after-the-other-rapid-succession from some sniper-perch.

And even beyond such sequential shit-will-happens . . . guns and their parts not discernable to metal detectors can be acquired . . . and with 3D printers and some programming skill, one can even produce his own "replacement plastic parts" even if aa traditional metal pistol, rifle, or other.

OHMYGOD !!!!
What are we to do?
How are we to do it?
Guns are "givens" (even when purchased . . or stolen . .) They're not going to go away or be taken away. But guns as deterrents to guns, though perhaps preemptively so, would not necessarily be but proliferations of "firefights" -- a situation readily imaged in that darkened theater. Shooter shoots, someone pulls a gun to take him down and someone else thinks the #2 is the bad guy and shoots him rather than the actual shooter (#1) and from the balcony ballistics bounce into the ground floor audience due to the darkness or bad aim or mistaken identity of #3 and #4, and #5 . . . . . all shooting to protect everyone from . . . each other???

So, you may argue, a school in session isn't in darkness. Good point. Personal gun possession as protection would generally be utilized by in situations where there'd be adequate lighting to see the bad guy.

But bad aim is "bad point" and what if, worst case scenario, the armed teacher, her hand shaking to confound her confused visual coordinates . . . what if she misses the shooter or even hits him and the bullet completely penetrates and plunges into a kid behind him?

IT SEEMS THAT THE MORE WE (OR AT LEAST I) THINK ABOUT EVERYTHING THERE IS TO THINK ABOUT IN THIS AREA OF WEAPONRY JEOPARDY, BUT PREVENTION AND PREEMPTION . . . . THE CLEARER IT IS THAT ANYONE HAVING A GUN THAT SHOOTS BULLETS IN EITHER AN ILLUSION OF INTERDICTORY INVOLVEMENT (TO STOP MASSACRE) OR MIGHT BE AN ACTUAL, THOUGH INADVERTENT, ACCIDENTAL "WHOOPS!!, Oh shit!!", ADDEND THERETO is packing the wrong kind of heat to preempt, protect, prevent, whatever of another's threat. Everyone armed isn't going to stop the so very few who commit gun atrocities. An armed populace as deterrent to a maniac with an automatic? Hell no. It's deranged or criminal people who kill, not guns. This would apply to "the people" if armed.

But, is there no solution?
So, is there no resolution?
Is it going to be that we just wait until the next "carnageval" comes to town? (carnage-carnival).

The solution and resolution first came to me back just after 9/11. Yes, as I said in my dissertations back then, and just above herein, -- had there been armed guards on either of those flights, there would have been dead terrorists before the planes were commandeered. But back then I considered that firing a gun, perhaps numerous rapid-succession times -- within a pressurized fuselage -- consisting of very thin and significantly aging if not fatigued metal -- might make for a "tear on dotted line" separation of the aircraft into parts. Yes, the bad guys would have been killed, the real estate spared, but the passengers would still have been killed by prior suck into the air or eventual smash into the ground.

It occurred to me in the context of this (granted semi-facetious) flight-fractionation scenario -- the astounding advantage of arming whomever, wherever . . . . not with guns of any kind that fire bullets . . .

. . . . but with guns that propel tranquilizer darts!!!!!!

Not much chance a tranquilizer dart would penetrate even the thin-residual-skin of an aircraft. If so, 'twould be but a "prick".

Mistake the Jordanian diplomat for one of the terrorists, shoot first. What's the harm?

And moving the venue to our present paradigms and premises of ponder . . .
In school or wherever, sense threat? Just shoot first!! Take down that assumed mass-killer even if he turns out to be the new janitor. He'll come to soon.

Teacher in actual assault situation pulls tranquilizer gun and shoots. Bad aim? Shoot again. I'm assuming that this new "generation" of tranquilizer weaponry will be at least semi-automatic". Take down a couple kids? No problem!! They'll come to soon, hardly the worse for wear. (Worst threat here, parental law suits of teacher and school and myriad other facets and factors involved in saving the life of their child -- such litigation a form of terrorism and atrocity itself!!!!!)

In darkened theater and someone shoots, who cares how many propel their tranquillizer darts into the murk. In fact, the more collapsed in temporary unconsciousness, the better. At least until it comes time to try to sort out who's who and extrapolate the lone villain from the volume of responders.

And maybe it would come to be that he'd be discovered, recognized, "outed" from the others . . . . because only the darts he'd fired would not just be tranquilizers . . . but also tipped with . . . p . . o . . . . . . i . . . . s . . . . o . . . . n . . .

So maybe the only safety is for everyone to be armed with . . . . . .

OR

THERE SHOULD BE HUMAN-DOSAGE-CALIBRATED TRANQUILIZER DARTS DEVELOPED. THERE SHOULD BE TRANQUILIZER GUNS STANDARD-ISSUED TO LAW ENFORCEMENT PERSONNEL INCLUDING EVEN SECURITY GUARDS.
(would have made a difference in that unfortunate Zimmerman v. Martin misunderstanding).
THERE SHOULD BE THAT PROTECTION FOR THOSE WHO PROTECT US -- TO SHOOT FIRST AND SORT OUT THE SHIT (and dna etc.) LATER WHEN THE THREAT HAS BEEN SECURED (cuffed, or whatever). SHOOT FIRST. IF IT WORKS WITH MASSIVE WILD ANIMALS IT SHOULD WORK WITH EVEN VERY LARGE FELLOW HUMANS.

SHOOT FIRST. NO HARM DONE.
But prior to issuing the devices and instituting the preemptive projectile procedure, LEGISLATE FIRST. IN ORDER TO PREVENT WHAT WOULD NO DOUBT OTHERWISE BE THE ATTACK OF THE LAWSUITS, THE LAWYERS. Against which the cops would have no protection.
Long ago I made this tranquilizer suggestion I THINK IT SHOULD BE AN IDEA DISCUSSED, PASSED ON, PROLIFERATED, INCORPORATED.

Regarding arming the public with a weapon that fires a non-lethal
but immediately disabling projectile. **The PRETT - GUN** (**pre**empt **t**he **t**hreat).

A proposal for a weapon to be provided for personal and professional (police, etc.) protection and preemption. "Shoot first!! Why not??" Arm the teachers in schools, even venue personnel otherwise. Why not *everyone* carry a PRETT?

This "gun" would allow someone to *"fire first, determine actual danger later"*. Thus even the threat of harm could be removed. Someone very
suspect could be "taken down" immediately. Any actualized threat, such as a school or theater shooter, or even terrorist, would be shot without thought --
by any of the many who would be armed with such a weapon.

My proposal is for a "semi-automatic" tranquilizer-dart gun (a single shot weapon wouldn't suffice against a conventionally armed murderer). A "six-shooter" (or even more "automatic") tranquilizer-dart gun should be feasible.

Combining existing design and manufacture process of 1) conventional guns (chamber, trigger, barrel, etc.), 2) construction nail gun propellant systems (compressed air, explosive mini-charge, or other), and 3) tranquilizer dart projectiles . . . . should be an easy manufacturing process.

Actual device would be the equivalent of a regular gun (pistol, rifle, etc.)
The cost of weapon should be equivalent to conventional gun, or less.
The tranquilizer-dart "ammunition" should already be available on the market that provides for biological and other scientific needs.

Arm the public for their safety: SHOOT FIRST!! Scrutinize later. No harm done. Just a period of unconsciousness for the suspect!!!! He'll come to.

God didn't create guns or it would have said so in Genesis.

But seriously, a serious study needs to be conducted, statistics recorded.
What proportion of populations in other countries have guns.
What is the socio-economic and age distribution of those populations.
What are the religious and ethnic demographics elsewhere.
Is ther any correlation between gun possession, gun crimes, and the above (other than, of course, where **no** guns there's no gun crime !!!)
Where (or if) population and police are not weaponized, is crime otherwise out of control? Is police gun possession a deterrent? Or exacerbation?
Is public possession a protection or an invitation to shoot-out mayhem, from individual rages to group rampages?

There's no conceivable possibility the American populace can be disarmed. The most draconian measures would result in insurrection even by those who are not actual gun-advocates.
Obviously, the crimes committed with guns are proportionate to the guns with which to commit. This holds true from the frontier days of the U. S. to the "frontiers" of elsewheres in the world today.
Gun control here is a delusion, though gun ownership requisites and registration are no more intrusive, or less important, than passing various tests before being able to drive a car, truck, or do potentially dangerous tasks and professions.

P, S, A factor over-riding fractional considerations is America's history as a nation. This is actually inherent in a significant "American mind-set" and literally documented (at least as far as "militia"-arms are concerned) in the Constitution. This heritage is different from other countries. Also, our "occupation" and conquest so suddenly and violently is somewhat unique -- and so much the gun was our forebears' banner marching into genocidal war.
Onward Christian soldiers . . . . . soldiers are armed.
Guns R Us.

Where there are more automobiles there will be more automobile accidents and injuries and deaths.
Where there are more sky divers there will be more deaths due to parachutes.
Where there are more ice cliff climbers there will be more deaths due to slipping and sliding and this variation on the theme of plummeting from on high.
Where there are more smokers there will be more emphesemaics and the cancerous.
Where there are more of anythings there will be more "stuff happens" happenings.
Except for automobiles, the above (and so many more) "stuffs of the disastrous happenings" have been, or at least could be somewhat controlled.

Per 100,000 population per region (urban, rural, American, different foreign) what number of deaths due to lightning, electrocution, drowning, autos, bikes, bicycles, overdoses of prescriptions, gas explosions, CO_2 poisoning, suicide, knifings, sexual exertion, medical error, . . . is the gun less dangerous than the gynecologist? or more significantly the surgeon? . . . . boating mishaps, sharks, spontaneous human combustion, snake bites, bat bites, dog bites, overbites, domestic violence with power tools, venomous pets, post traumatic stress disorder, postal workers, Monsanto Corporation, Monopoly game disputes, falling architectural elements, falling in general (on ice, in tubs, off whatever) . . . . . .

According to the National Highway Traffic Administration, car accidents happen every minute of the day. Motor vehicle accidents occur in any part of the world every 60 seconds. And if it's all summed up in a yearly basis, there are 5.25 million driving accidents that take place per year. Statistics show that each year,43,000 or more of the United States' population die due to vehicular accidents and around 2.9 million people end up suffering light or severe injuries. In a certain five year period, there had been recorded a 25% of the driving population who encountered or were involved in car accidents. It is also affirmed that car accidents kill a child every 3 minutes. Statistics on the number of car accidents taking place in every state or country is normally based on medical or insurance records filed.

Based on a research conducted years back, an estimated number of 1.2 million car accident deaths occurred last 2004 and 50 million people injured worldwide. In the Global Status Report on Road Safety 2009 made by the World Health Organization, more than 90% of the world's road casualties happen in low and middle income countries which comprise only 48% of the world's registered vehicles. The escalating death rates pertaining to driving accidents over the years have already become one of the most serious global issues. It is estimated that by 2020, road accident casualties will exceed HIV/AIDS mortality and disability rate.

There were several legislative amendments and technical changes made such as brakes innovation to reduce fatal accident rates but the contributing factors to vehicular accidents especially driver impairment or behavior surmounted. **The factors that contribute to roadway accidents are mostly preventable and only require reasonable care.** In a study concerning car crashes, it shows that the ultimate contributing factor in vehicular accidents is driver impairment or error such as poor eyesight, phone distractions and drunk driving. Other road accident contributing factors are traffic violations, equipment or vehicle failure and road conditions.

Driving accidents are also considered the ultimate cause of permanent disability of in most countries. These tragic accidents take the lives of thousands of people while millions of surviving vehicular accident victims suffers from injuries and permanent disabilities on the part of those who are severely hurt. The aftermath of vehicular accidents aside from bodily injuries or death is the financial damage which is suffered by the parties involved. The financial burden as a result of car damages and the loss of income or wage typically involves a great deal of money. It is the paramount interest of the state to protect the safety of its people and although numerous precautionary measures are taken to prevent or lessen car accident related deaths, this will always be a long term global concern if people will not constantly practice the discipline required to ensure safety.

If not blinded by the Amendment entitlement threat paranoia of this sacred stuff (personal weapons), anyone should realize that where it's at is where there are more guns there will be more gun accidents and assaults and injuries and deaths and murders (even "mass-".). This would include that where there are fewer law enforcement fire arms, there will be fewer deaths resulting from police "shootality" (too often, it seems, a factor of brutality which leads to mob "retaliality").

In the United Kingdom and Wales, also New Zealand, the regular cops don't have guns. Only "special forces" have actual fire-arms. Over a recent two-year period in the U.K. there were no deaths resulting from police shootings.

Of proportionate note are the number of guns amongst the populace and the number of crimes and shootings that result. Obviously in a realm of no guns there would be no gun crimes committed. I hardly need to repeat that, though I just have.

In the following information, primarily researched on the Internet, I provide only a sample of what should be a comprehensive perspective upon which anyone determines whether guns should be banned or to what extent controlled. It should be self-evident, self-explanatory, self-sufficient proof that "un possession is inversely proportionate to gun problems" . . . . is a false conclusion – other than within certain areas such as big cities. In some regions of the country, just about everyone has firearms, yet there are negligible firearm casualties of any sort (other than to game animals).

UNODC murder rates for recent years

Region	rate per 100,000	count
Americas (No & So)	16.3	157,000
Africa	12.5	135,000
World	6.2	437,000
Europe	3.0	22,000
Oceania	3.0	1,100
Asia	2.9	122,000

China and United Kingdom – public possession of fire arms banned

Australia, Japan, Singapore – strict and difficult requirements
Canada – must be registered and have training and personal risk assessment, criminal background check, and two references

High income countries averaged 1.66 million crimes in 2002
        Eurozone average --   980,998.22
        Emerging markets average –   743,210.43

States

As of 2012, 13 of the 14 "battleground states" - gun ownership 30% or more. All ten of them with highest gun ownership (50% or more) are Republican. Nine of the ten states with the lowest gun ownership (all less than 30%) are Dem., sole exception being Florida, a "battleground state" with 24.5 gun ownership.

Honduras, far fewer guns but highest 68/100,000 gun murders.
US - highest per capita gun ownership but gun homicides 3/100,000
Variance of gun ownership by state

US STATE	crime rating	POPULA-TION	% gun owners	murders / 100 th	by gun	college grad	% white
Wash. DC	13.9	604,723	3.6	21.8	16.5	65.6	38.5
Louisiana	10.8	4,533,572	44.1	9.6	7.7	20.5	62.6
New Mexico	6,6	2,059,179	34.8	5.7	3.3	24.8	68.4
Maryland	6.3	5,773,552	21.3	7.3	5.1	35.2	58.2
Tennessee	6.0	6.346,105	43.9	5.6	3.5	21.8	77.6
Alabama	7.1	4,779,736	51.7	4.2	2.8	21.4	68.5
Mississippi	7.4	2,967,297	55.3	5.6	4.0	18.9	59.1
Missouri	6.5	5,988,927	41.7	7.0	6.4	24.5	82.8
Michigan	7.0	9.993,640	38.4	5.6	4.2	24.7	78.9
S Carolina	6.9	4,625,364	42.3	6.1	4.5	23.5	66.2
Arkansas	5.9	2,915,918	55.3	4.5	3.2	19.3	77
Oklahoma	5.7	3,751,351	42.9	5.0	3.0	22.6	72.2
Illinois	5.8	12,830,632	20.2	3.5	2.8	29.5	71.3
Nevada	4.5	2,700,551	33.8	6.9	3.1	21.8	66.2

Georgia	5.9	9,920,000	40.3	5.3	3.8	27.1	59.7
Florida	5.2	19,687,653	24.5	5.0	3.9	25.8	75
Arizona	5.5	6,392,017	31.1	5.5	3.6	26.0	73
Texas	4.4	25.145.561	35.9	5.0	3.2	25.2	70.4
California	5.0	37,253,956	21.3	4.9	3.4	29.5	57.6
N Carolina	4.9	9,535,483	41.3	4.7	3.0	25.6	68.5
Pennsylvania	5.4	12,702,279	34.7	5.1	3.6	25.8	81.9
Indiana	4.7	6,483,802	39.1	3.1	2.2	22.1	84.3
Delaware	6.2	893,934	25.5	5.3	6.2	26.1	68.9
W Virginia	3.9	6,724,540	33.1	2.2	1.4	17.3	93.9
Ohio	4.3	11,536,504	32.4	4.0	2.7	24.1	82.7
Virginia	3.8	8,001,024	35.1	4.6	3.1	33.6	68.6
Kansas	2.9	2,853,118	42.1	3.5	2.2	28.8	83.8
Kentucky	4.5	4,339,367	47.7	4.6	2.7	20.0	87.8
New York	3.5	19,378,102	18.0	4.4	2.7	31.7	65.7
New Jersey	4.4	8,791,894	12.3	4,1	2,7	33.9	68.6
Colorado	3.1	5,029,196	34.7	2.3	1.3	35.0	81.3
Alaska	4.1	710,231	57.8	4.4	2.7	21.4	66.7
Connecticut	4.1	3,574,097	16.7	3.7	2.7	34.7	77.8
Montana	2.7	989,415	57.7	2.1	1.2	27.0	89.4
Rhode Isl.	3.2	1,052,567	12.8	2.8	1.5	29.8	81.4
Washington	3.0	6,724,540	33.1	2.2	1.4	30.3	77.3
Massachusetts	1.8	6,547,629	12.6	3,2	1,8	37.9	80.4
So. Dakota	3.0	814,180	56.6	1.7	1.0	25.0	85.9
Wisconsin	3.0	5,686,986	44.4	2.7	1.7	25.4	86.2
Wyoming	2.4	536,626	59.7	1.4	.9	23.4	35.4
Nebraska	2.9	1,826,341	38.6	2.8	1.8	27.5	86.1
Oregon	2.4	3,831,074	39.8	2.0	.9	28.3	83.6
Maine	1.9	2,328,361	40.5	1.8	.8	26.7	95.2
Hawaii	2.1	???					
No Dakota	4.0	672,591	50.7	1.3	.6	25.7	90
Idaho	1.6	1,567,582	55.3	1.3	.8	24.5	89.1
Minnesota	1.8	5,303,925	41.7	1.7	1.0	31.0	85.3
Utah	1.8	2,763,885	43.9	1.9	.8	28.7	86.1
Iowa	1.6	3,036,355	42.9	1.2	.7	24.3	91.3
Vermont	1.3	625,741	42.0	1.1	.3	33.6	99.3
New Hamp	1.1	1,316,470	30.0	1.0	,4	32.5	93.9
Wyoming	2.4	563,626	59.7	1.4	.9	23.4	90.7
Montana	2.9	989,415	57.7	2.1	1.2	27.0	89.4

"The pattern is staggering. A number of U. S. cities have gun homicide rates in line with the most deadly nations in the world.

If a country: New Orleans (rate of 62.1 gun murders per 100,000) would rank second in the world.

Detroit	35.9	would rank a little less than El Salvador	39.0
Baltimore	29.7		Guatamala	34.8
Cleveland	17.3		Dominican Rep	16.3
Newark	25.4		Colombia	27.1
Buffalo	16.5		Panama	16.2
Miami	23.7		Colombia	27.1
Houston	12.9		Ecuador	12.7
Washington DC	19		Brazil	18.1
Chicago	11.6		Guyana	11.5
Atlanta	17.2		So Africa	17.0
Phoenix	10.6		Mexico	10.0
Los Angeles	9.2		Philippines	8.9
Boston	6.2		Nicaragua	5.9
New York	4		Argentina	3

Society and Culture > Crime & Law Enforcement > Crime Data

Murder Victims, by Weapons Used

The following table shows the number and percent of murder victims in the United States by the cause of death. Weapons used or cause of death include guns, stabbing, blunt objects, strangulation, arson, and more.

Weapons used or cause of death

Year	Murder victims, total	Guns Total	Percent	Cutting or stabbing	Blunt object	Strangulation, hands, fists, feet, or pushing	Arson	All other
1965	8,773	5,015	57.2%	2,021	505	894	226	112
1970	13,649	9,039	66.2	2,424	604	1,031	353	198
1975	18,642	12,061	64.7	3,245	1,001	1,646	193	496
1980	21,860	13,650	62.0	4,212	1,094	1,666	291	947
1985	17,545	10,296	58.7	3,694	972	1,491	243	849
1990	20,045	12,847	64.1	3,503	1,075	1,424	287	909
1991	21,676	14,373	66.3	3,430	1,099	1,529	195	847
1992	22,716	15,489	68.2	3,296	1,040	1,445	203	1,043
1993	23,180	16,136	69.6	2,967	1,022	1,482	217	1,168
1994	22,084	15,463	70.0	2,802	912	1,452	196	1,079
1995	20,232	13,790	68.2	2,557	918	1,438	166	968
1996	15,848	10,744	67.8	2,142	733	1,182	151	726
1997	15,289	10,369	67.8	1,963	702	1,187	134	934
2002	14,263	9,528	66.7	1,776	681	954	103	874
2006	14,990	10,177	67.9	1,822	607	833	115	1,128
2007	14,831	10,086	68.0	1,796	647	854	130	1,016
2008	14,224	9,528	66.9	1,888	603	964	85	1,156
2011	12,795	8,653	67.6	1,716	502	751	76	1,009
2012	12,765	8,855	69.4	1,589	518	767	85	951

ead more: Murder Victims, by Weapons Used http://www.infoplease.com/ipa/A0004888.html#ixzz3XIUKvQpR

Per vehicle mile travelled, motorcyclists' risk of a fatal crash is 35 times greater than a passenger car

According to the U.S. National Highway Traffic Safety

Administration (NHTSA), in 2006, 13.10 cars out of 100,000 ended up in fatal crashes. The rate for motorcycles is 72.34 per 100,000 registered motorcycles.[1] Motorcycles also have a higher fatality rate per unit of distance travelled when compared with automobiles.

In 2004, figures from the UK Department for Transport indicated that motorcycles have 16 times the rate of serious injuries per 100 million vehicle kilometers compared to cars, and double the rate of bicycles.

Since 1980, motorcycle ownership among rider
riders in 1980 to 43.7 percent in 1998. The mean
also increased, from an average engine size of
24.7 percent. This combination of older riders c
increase in motorcycle deaths from the late 199

Half of motorcycle fatalities in single vehicle cr
percent of motorcyclist fatalities in single vehic

In 2009, motorcycle fatalities in the US declined
Automobile fatalities continued to decline for th
the late-2000s recession might account for the dec
Safety Association, but a State motorcyclists' rights or
increased, influenced by motorcycles' better fuel econ

Year	Fatalities
1996	2,161
1997	2,116
1998	2,294
1999	2,483
2000	2,897
2001	3,197†
2002	3,244
2003	3,661‡
2004	4,028
2005	4,576
2006	4,837
2007	5,174
2008	5,312
2009	4,462
2010	3,615

† some NHTSA lists show 3,181
‡ some NHTSA lists show 3,714

Unintentional drowning is the third leading cause of unintentional injury resulting in death worldwide. In 2013 it was down from 545,000 deaths in 1990. Of these deaths, 82,000 occurred in children less than five years old. It accounts for 7
5 of all injury related deaths (excluding natural disasters), with 96% of these deaths occurring in low-income and middle-income countries In many countries, drowning is one of the leading causes of death for children under 12 years old. For example, in the United States, it is the second leading cause of death (after motor vehicle crashes) in children 12 and younger. The rate of drowing in populations around the world varie widely according to their access to water, the climate, and the national swimming culture.

less than five years old.[5] It accounts for 7% of all injury related deaths (excluding those due to natural disasters), with 96% of these deaths occurring in low-income and middle-income countries.[6] In many countries, drowning is one of the leading causes of death for children under 12 years old. For example, in the United States, it is the second leading cause of death (after motor vehicle crashes) in children 12 and younger.[2] The rate of drowning in populations around the world varies widely according to their access to water, the climate and the national swimming culture.

Over 17,000 people die from falls each

year. That's a 1 in 218 chance over your lifetime,

compared to a 1 in 3,700,000 chance of being killed by a shark.

TOP 5 CAUSES OF ACCIDENTAL DEATH IN THE UNITED STATES

[HOMEMISCELLANEOUS](#)TOP 5 CAUSES OF ACCIDENTAL DEATH IN THE UNITED STATES

Accidents happen — and they also kill enough people to rank as the No. 1 cause of death for those ages 1 to 42, according to the National Safety Council. Accidents are the fifth-leading cause of death across all age groups, topped only by a spate of illnesses that include heart disease and cancer. And it's not the heavy-machinery operators, high-rise window washers or electricians who most frequently succumb to fatal accidents. The vast majority of accidental deaths happen at home or in the community — not at work — with the top five causes often stemming from routine activities.

5. Choking (Approximately 2,500 deaths per year)

Photo credit: Jovan Nikolic/Shutterstock.com

Hot dogs can be a quick, easy — and deadly — meal. Hot dogs are the perfect size, shape and consistency to block a child's airway, and a WebMd report rates hot dogs as the top choking hazard for children. Choking killed about 2,500 people in 2009, according to the National Safety Council, and kids ages 3 and under are at the highest risk. Potential choking hazards include balloons, marshmallows, gooey gel candies, grapes, nuts, chewing gum, carrots, chunks of meat and peanut butter, apples, hard, round candies and small toys kids like to put in their mouths. Reduce your child's risk of choking by cutting up foods into very small pieces and closely monitoring your children while eating, especially if they are eating while walking, laughing or fooling around.

4. Fires (2,700 annual deaths)

Photo credit: Ronald Caswell/Shutterstock.com

A smoking gun isn't the only thing that can kill — smoking, flaming and burning homes typically kill thousands of folks each year. Deaths from residential fires in the United States dropped to a five-year low in 2009, with 2,480, but a good chunk of them probably could have been avoided. Smoking is the cause behind some 450 of the fire deaths annually, according to the U.S. Fire Administration, while other "careless" causes result in another 400 deaths each year. So blow out that candle. Another 80 or so yearly deaths are the result of fires in non-residential buildings. Public safety initiatives to get fire alarms installed and regularly checked in all residential dwellings has cut the number of deaths from fires by roughly one-third in the past 20 years.

3. Falls (25,000 annual deaths)

Forbis/Shutterstock.com

Falls into the Grand Canyon may make the headlines, but falls around the home are the ones killing people at an alarming rate. Falls killed about 25,000 people in 2009, according to the National Safety Council, with those over age 65 making up the vast majority of the victims. In fact, falls are the leading cause of injury death for folks age 65 and older, the Centers for Disease Control reports, as well as their most common cause of nonfatal injuries and hospitalization for trauma. Death rates from falls among those 65 and older have also skyrocketed in the past decade, although the CDC does not say why. Kids fall, too, but they usually don't die from it. Home and playground falls are the leading cause of nonfatal injuries for children up to age 19. Supervising kids, reducing home tripping risks and regular exercise for older adults can lower the fall risk.

2. Poisoning (39,000 annual deaths)

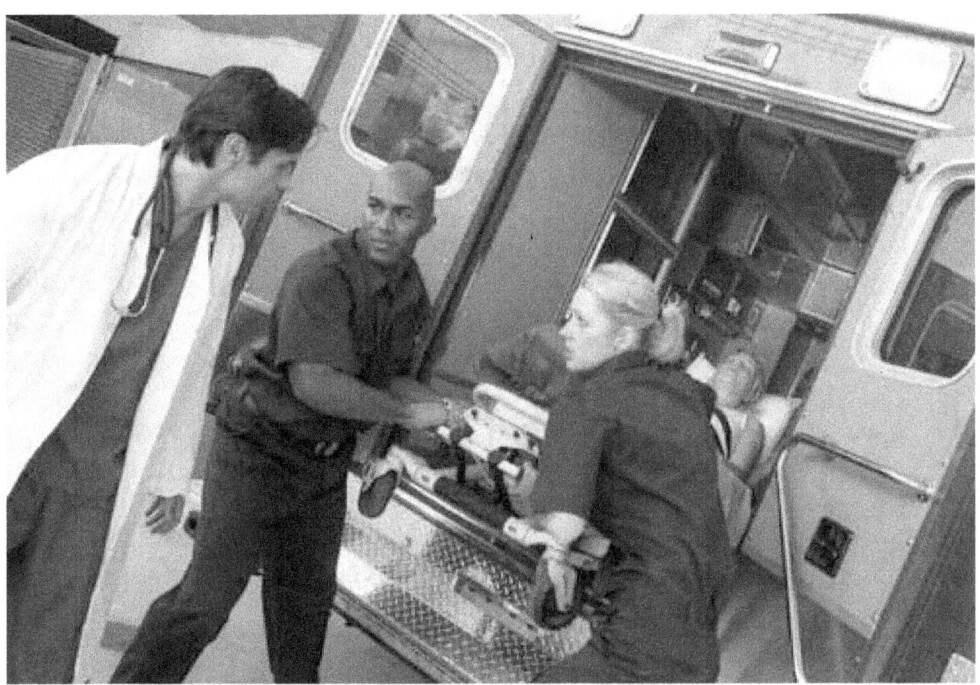
Photo credit: Monkey Business Images/Shutterstock.com

There's a reason people warn against abusing drugs — it kills you. Poisoning killed nearly 40,000 people in 2009, according to the National Safety Council, with most of the deaths associated with the accidental ingestion of illegal drugs. The number of deaths is up almost 400 percent in the past 20 years. Perhaps surprisingly, children getting into kitchen solvents or grandma's well-stocked medicine cabinets are not the ones dying at alarming rates. Adults ages 25 to 44 are subject to the highest poisoning death rates, followed closely by those in the 45 to 64 age group. Drugs account for more than 10 times the amount of poisoning deaths of all other substances, according to the Centers for Disease Control. Top culprits are opioid pain medications, such as oxycodone, hydrocodone and methadone, with cocaine and heroin ranked second and third. Alcohol poisoning exists, but its numbers are so comparatively low it barely makes a blip on the National Safety Council's poisoning death chart.

1. Motor Vehicle Incidents (42,000 annual deaths)

Photo credit: Jeff Thrower/Shutterstock.com

If motorists would stop texting, cell-phone yakking, applying makeup and eating while driving, we'd surely have fewer than the 36,000 deaths associated with motor vehicle crashes the National Safety Council reported for 2009. Distracted driving is the No. 1 offender and young adults are the No. 1 offenders, with their fatal crash rate three times higher than any other age group. But don't think you can breathe easy just because you are over age 21. While vehicle crashes are the leading cause of death for 15- to 20-year-olds, the crashes young drivers cause kill people in all age groups. So hang up that cell-phone call, stop texting in the intersection and buckle that seat belt, all of which can reduce your death risk considerably. Oh, and don't drink and drive. Alcohol is involved in about 32 percent of fatal crashes across the board.

The 42,000 annual deaths noted above include some 5,000 annual pedestrian fatalities — most the result of motor-vehicle incidents — and several hundred fatalities attributed to vehicle/bicycle collisions, according to the Centers For Disease Control.

One More: Drowning (2,000 annual deaths)

Photo credit: Pies 721/Shutterstock.com

The adage is true: children can, in fact, drown in as little as 1 inch of water. Add an unmanned, unfenced and much deeper swimming pool into the equation and you have yourself a very deadly mix. Approximately 2,000 people drowned in 2009, the National Safety Council reports, with the Centers for Disease Control noting that drowning is the leading cause of injury death for children ages 1 to 4. Life jackets, pool fences and knowing CPR can help save lives, as can taking a gander around the home for other drowning hazards. Bathtubs — even those with baby seats or supportive devices — pose a huge risk, as do buckets, hot tubs, ice chests containing melted ice and toilets. That childproof toilet lid latch is not a joke. Drowning hazards outside the home include irrigation ditches, wells, fountains, fish ponds and even a small and shallow post hole, provided it has at least 1 inch of water.

Postscript: Accidental Shootings (600 annual deaths)

Sports injury statistics
How frequently do sports injuries occur?

Photo credit: Gualberto Becerra/Shutterstock.com

Kids and guns don't mix, especially when those guns are carelessly left in unlocked cabinets or even in plain view. Accidental shootings resulted in 642 deaths in 2009, placing them seventh on this list. Firearms are the second-leading cause of non-natural deaths for kids, typically from a gun the kid finds somewhere around the house, according to a University of Utah report that mentioned additional horrific statistics. About two-thirds of accidental shooting deaths happen in the home, with the kid shooting himself to death in 45 percent of the cases and friends or family members pulling the trigger in the remainder. More than 50 percent of American households have a gun in the house, and, in one survey, 10 percent said they had loaded firearms in unlocked locations that were easily accessible to kids. There is obviously a need to keep guns in locked, inaccessible and child-resistant locations and store them unloaded.

In the United States, about 30 million children and teens participate in some form of organized sports, and about 3 million injuries each year, which cause some loss of time of participation, are experienced by the participants. Almost one-third of all injuries incurred in childhood are sports-related injuries. By far, the most common injuries are sprains and strains.

Obviously, some sports are more dangerous than others. For example, contact sports such as football can be expected to result in a higher number of injuries than a non-contact sport such as swimming. However, all types of sports have a potential for injury, whether from the trauma of contact with other players or from overuse or misuse of a body part.

Injury statistics and incidence rates:

The following statistics are the latest available from the National Safe Kids

Campaign and the American Academy of Pediatrics (AAP):

Injury rates:

Approximately 3 million children ages 14 and under get hurt annually playing sports or participating in recreational activities.

Although death from a sports injury is rare, the leading cause of death from a sports-related injury is a brain injury.

Sports and recreational activities contribute to approximately 21 percent of all traumatic brain injuries among American children.

The majority of head injuries sustained in sports or recreational activities occur during bicycling, skateboarding, or skating incidents.

More than 775,000 children, ages 14 and under, are treated in hospital emergency rooms for sports-related injuries each year. Most of the injuries occurred as a result of falls, being struck by an object, collisions, and overexertion during unorganized or informal sports activities.

Where and when:

- Playground- and bicycle-related injuries occur most often among young children, between the ages of 5 and 9 years old. Bicycle- and sports-related injuries also affect older children, in addition to overexertion.
- The highest rates of injury occur in sports that involve contact and collisions.
- More severe injuries occur during individual sports and recreational activities.
- Most organized sports-related injuries (60 percent) occur during practice.

Who:

- Almost 6 million high school children participate in team sports.
- Children between 5 and 14 years of age account for almost half (40 percent) of sports-related injuries for all age groups.
- Approximately 20 million children take part in recreational or competitive sports outside of school.
- Approximately 20 percent of children participating in sports activities are injured each year, and one in four injuries is considered serious.

- Children who are less developed than a more mature child of the same age and weight are at increased risk for injury.
- Severity of sports-related injuries increases with age.
- Before puberty, girls and boys suffer the same risk of sports injuries.
- During puberty, boys suffer more severe injuries than girls.
- Children who are just beginning a sport or activity are at greater risk for injury.

Types of sports and recreational activities:

Consider the following statistics:

- Basketball - In 1998, nearly 200,000 children ages 5 to 14 were treated in hospital emergency rooms for basketball-related injuries. The majority of the injured children (70 percent) were boys.
- Baseball and softball - In 1998, more than 91,000 children ages 5 to 14 were treated in hospital emergency rooms for baseball-related injuries, and nearly 26,000

children ages 5 to 14 were treated for softball-related injuries.

- Bicycling - In 1998, more than 320,000 children ages 5 to 14 were treated in hospital emergency rooms for bicycle-related injuries. In addition, 225 children ages 14 and under died in bicycle-related crashes in 1997.

- Football - In 1998, more than 159,000 children ages 5 to 14 were treated in hospital emergency rooms for football-related injuries.

- Gymnastics - In 1998, nearly 25,500 children ages 5 to 14 were treated in hospital emergency rooms for gymnastics-related injuries. Among girls' sports, gymnastics has one of the highest injury rates, increasing with the level of competition.

- Ice skating - In 1998, more than 15,500 children ages 5 to 14 were treated in hospital emergency rooms for ice skating-related injuries.

- In-line skating/roller skating - Since 1992, 33 children ages 14 and under have died from in-line skating injuries, mostly from collisions with motor vehicles. In 1998, more than 67,000 children ages 5 to 14 were treated in hospital emergency rooms for in-line skating-related injuries while more than 32,000 children ages 5 to 14 were treated in hospital emergency rooms for roller-skating-related injuries.

- Skateboarding - In 1998, more than 27,500 children ages 5 to 14 were treated in hospital emergency rooms for skateboarding-related injuries.

- Sledding - In 1998, nearly 8,500 children ages 5 to 14 were treated in hospital emergency rooms for sledding-related injuries.

- Snow skiing/snowboarding - In 1997, more than 13,500 children ages 5 to 14 were treated in hospital emergency rooms for snow skiing-related injuries. Another 9,000 children ages 5 to 14 were treated in hospital emergency rooms for snowboarding-related injuries.

- Soccer - In 1998, more than 77,500 children ages 5 to 14 were treated in hospital emergency rooms for soccer-related injuries.

- Trampolines - In 1998, more than 75,000 children ages 14 and under were treated in hospital emergency rooms for trampoline-related injuries. Most trampoline injuries occur at home (90 percent) and involve injury to a child's extremities.

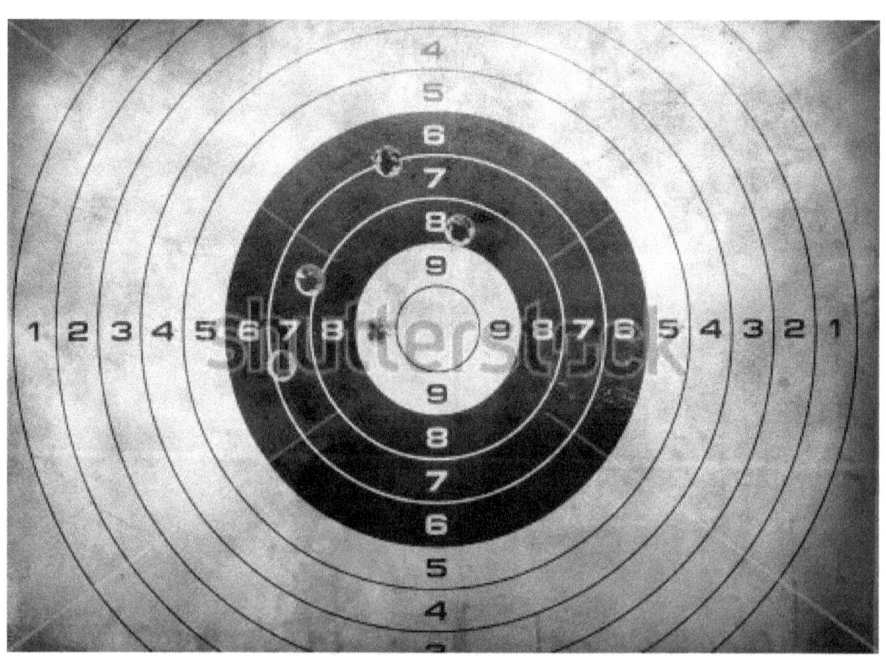

YES, A LOT OF PEOPLE GET KILLED BY GUNS. A LOT OF KIDS, SOME OF THEM ACCIDENTALLY SHOOTING EACH OTHER. GUNS ARE DANGEROUS IF THEY'RE NOT HANDLED BY COMPETENT, SANE, MATURE PEOPLE. GUNS INJURE AND KILL. SO FAR I'VE CONSIDERED THE SITUATION IN THE UNITED STATES.

IT SEEMS TO ME THAT THAT THE ACTUAL, STATISTICAL, CORRELATION OF GUN INJURIES AND DEATHS ARE

NOT PROPORTIONATE TO THE POPULATION THAT POSSESSES GUNS. OVERALL !! THE WESTERN AND NORTHERN STATES ARE CERTAINLY GUN TOTING STATES. BUT DON'T SEE CARNAGE GOING ON AMONGST THE RESIDENT - PACKERS OF HEAT.

WHERE THE NUMBER OF GUNS AND THE NUMBER OF GUNNED DOWN (OR HELD UP BY) IS A DIRECT PROPORTION IS IN THE DEPRESSED AREAS OF THE CITIES. BUT TAKE AWAY ALL THEIR SATURDAY NIGHT SPECIALS
AND WOULD THERE NOT BE NEXT A LOT OF SLICING GOING ON??

AND WOULD THERE THEN COME TO BE AN OUTCRY ABOUT BLADED DEVICES AND THE ADVENT OF A "KNIFE LOBBY" (the NKA)?

To criminalize private ownership of firearms would be impossible, futile, counterproductive, counterintuitive. More carnage takes place by drunken drivers, just incompetent drivers, dangerous activities, and natural

phenomena than by guns. Yes, if all guns could be gone, there'd no longer be ANY gun violence. But other than some drastic, medieval, or Mid-eastern, paradigm of punishment for firearm possession, ... even if such were instated, there'd the guns . .
. . .

Regarding gun ownership and gun owners, heaven forbid the ignorance, let alone futility, of any attempt to disarm the armed populace of this country. Aside from the Constitutional entitlement and guarantee, basic brain behavior should reveal that in a world of weapons' threats (perhaps so far just latent) abroad -- as well as sporadically domestic . . . . actually being without any means of self-defense may represent group naiveté, though maybe not quite stupidity.
Some time or other ago I posted a couple discourses shortly following the Connecticut school shooting. I thought I comprehensively presented a rational analysis of gun issues, including my conclusion that getting trying to get rid of guns would accomplish weapons-worsenings (a la Prohibition).

I'm all in favor of gun ownership. A gun in one's home could very well be equivalent to a "fire-power extinguisher" (should there come an armed intruder . . or eventually insurgent force) . . An actual fire extinguisher to put out actual flames should also be part of one's protection (and I would think required, if not by law, by insurance companies!!!!)
I feel that the gun lobby can be faulted for its abject resistance to registering gun owners, & to some format of background check prior to passing the pistol or other over the counter. Think of the myriad situations (driver's license, insurance, hospital volunteer positions . . . .) that require background screening of the applicant's suitability for whatever. The "Gun Lobby Ludicry" may be that, given its unquestionable influence/clout, it doesn't "legitimize" (even "elevate") its demographic and legislative stance by establishing its own criteria. Thus gun-owners would become an "echelon of the qualified!!!"

I've never owned a gun. But if I were appraised that within X period of time the opportunity for one to purchase a weapon would end, but ownership would be "grandfathered", I'd hasten out to procure one!!!
That's as simply as I can state my position on ownership per se. For me 'twould be a pistol.

Regarding types of weapon . . . another of my issues taken issue with . . . I should think the gun lobby itself would back bans on the ballistic baddies . . . military-style assault weapons -- unless, by specific licensing, for specific "extreme-target" competitions (for example). What rationale, what justification for legal 100-round/seconds (+/-) firepower of a rifle when there's no outcry of threatened autonomy or 2nd Amend. "confiscation" concerning someone owning a bazooka or grenade?

As far as there being "bumps in the road" to impede what I've written previously, I thought I'd leveled the length and breadth of the lanes we travel. Criminalizing whatever, adds criminality to such other concerns (so often subjective) as ethics or morality, kind of synergizing "sin" -- and locking it up in contexts and confines such that the penal system may be the worse crime committed!!

Heaven forbid Sharia -- or Puritan "purity" and punishments -- though such cruelty might equal control.
But some regulation, registration, seems necessary to assure the Constitutional right of the "pursuit of self-preservation" of all Americans.
Or should we do away with all testing and licensing because that might lead to the government taking away our motorcycles . . . . ?

regarding the proposed weapon registration bill and response thereto by Cpl Joshua Boston

(this "went viral" on the internet a couple years ago.)

To Senator Dianne Feinstein,

I will not register my weapons should this bill be passed, as I do not believe it is the government's right to know what I own. Nor do I think it prudent to tell you what I own so that it may be taken from me by a group of people who enjoy armed protection yet decry me having the same a crime. You ma'am have overstepped a line that is not your domain. I am a Marine Corps Veteran of 8 years, and I will not have some woman who proclaims the evil of an inanimate object, yet carries one, tell me I may not have one.

I am not your subject. I am the man who keeps you free. I am not your servant. I am the person whom you serve. I am not your peasant. I am the flesh and blood of America. I am the man who fought for my country. I am the man who learned. I am an American. You will not tell me that I must register my semi-automatic AR-15 because of the actions of some evil man.

I will not be disarmed to suit the fear that has been established by the media and your misinformation campaign against the American public.

We, the people, deserve better than you.

Respectfully Submitted,
Joshua Boston
Cpl, United States Marine Corps
2004-2012

My response to the above (which I posted on a blog site but it didn't go viral, thankfully, for someone probably would have shot me for what I wrote).

Please understand that I thank and admire Cpl Joshua for his
service as a Marine. And I respect the sincerity and recognize
the emotional validity of his response to the proposed gun bill.
And please allow my contrasting, even in points conflicting, response to him.

Joshua seems proud to have served his country as a Marine.
Considering his relation to his country otherwise, his distrust and
     disrespect for his country represents sedition. Such a stance with
     regard to some order or regulation in the Corps would have been
     a punishable offence, possibly unto court marshal.
The President of the United States is the Commander-in chief of the Military.
    The government of the United States is his "chain of command" so to speak. Laws
    are passed by the government within context and constituent ranks
    of the President (so to speak).
        Cpl. Joshua is blatantly stating his refusal to obey his commander in chief!!

> *"I will not register my weapons should this bill be passed, as I do not
> believe it is the government's right to know what I own. Nor do I think
> it prudent to tell you what I own so that it may be taken from me by a
> group of people who enjoy armed protection yet decry me the same
> a crime."*

    As a citizen of this country, all the more as a member of the Marine Corp or other
        armed services of this country, it is not one's singular right to supervene,
        by evasion or rebellion or insurrection, the consensus/legislated rules and
        laws of governance of this country.
            There is not a proposal to confiscate anyone's legally owned
        weapons.
            There is a need to control just who can own what kind of weapon –
        or would it be the *"you, ma'am have overstepped a line that is not*
        your domain. I am a Marine Corps Veteran of 8 years, and I will
        not have some woman who proclaims the evil of an inanimate
        object, yet carries one, tell me I may not have . . . ." a bazooka,
        a Sherman tank, a live hand grenade, a machine gun, a nuke!!!

> *"I am not your subject. I am the man who keeps you free. I am not
> your <u>servant</u>. I am the person you serve. I am not your <u>peasant</u>."*

     What possible relation does this have to a proposal for some kind
     of control over who possesses what devices (guns) that have no
     other purpose of design or use than collection, target practice,
     crime, or killing??

In registering an automobile does one act as a "servant"?
In filling out forms and providing information for everything from insurance to internet to bank account is one a "peasant"?

"I am not your servant. I am the person you serve." ??????

No one has proposed taking away anyone's guns.
The idea is to have at least a little control over who gets what kind of guns.

     Cpl. Joshua, what if one of those kids in that theater or the Connecticut school had been your son or daughter?? Or, in order not to seem insecure almost unto paranoia, and hypocritical as well . . . . perhaps you should proclaim your rights of refusal to register to vote or drive or bank or go online and you'd better stop paying taxes for all these categories resulting from regulations actually **require that you give up something (such as fees, charges, taxes).**

     Registering your semi-automatic probably would require only your signature.
     You are the man who fought for your country? Why then are you fighting against it now?
     You are an American? Yet you're telling America that your private/personal premise takes priority?
           . . . . . .even when the protection of your fellow-Americans is involved?

     You are a Marine. You served your country. It didn't serve you -- except chow.

"I will not be disarmed to suit the fear that has been established by the media and your misinformation campaign against the American people." The fear was established by lunatics with semiautomatic weapons, not the media. That insufficient control of gun purchase exists to keep such massacre-tragedies from happening . . . is this "misinformation".

"**. . . . .against the American people . . .**" The campaign here is Joshua's.

Read his "the pending Feinstein gun bill . . . and a response . . ." piece carefully, analytically.

It used to be . . .my country, right or wrong . . . . but we've come down to the primacy-priority:

. . . . .MY GUNS RIGHT OR WRONG . . . . . .

.

THE MOST EFFECTIVE ADVERTISING FOR GUN POSSESSION ..

ELSEWHERE IN THE WORLD

Homicide rate: intentional global homicide rate of 7.6 per 100,000 (2004)
Includes other than gun murders (infanticide, assisted suicide, euthanasia, etc.)

Composite: Americas 16.3 – Africa 12.4 – Europe 3.0 – Oceania 3.0 – Asia 2.9

	Pop	med. age	fert.rate	/km	urban pop.	gun/100 Pop.	repro	prison/ 100,000
China	1,39 bil	35.7	1.66	145	54%	4.9	1	172
India	1,27	26.6	2.53	386	32	4.2	5.0	30
USA	323 mil	27.5	1.99	34	83	90	4.7	707
Pakistan	185	22.8	3.3	233	37	11.6	8	41
Nigeria	179 mil	17.8	6.01	193	51	.7	20	33
Bangladesh	159	25.4	2.24	1101	30	.5	2.7	45
Russia	143	38.4	1.51	8	74	8.9	9.2	470
Japan	127	46.2	1.4	336	93	6	.3	51
Mexico	124	27.3	2.73	63	79	15	21.5	211
Philippines	100	23.2	4.72	334	50	4.7	8.8	113
Ethiopia	97	18.4	4.72	87	18	4.0	12	111
Vietnam	93	30.3	1.78	279	33	1.7	3.3	143
Egypt	83	25.5	2.82	83	44	3.5	3.4	76
Germany	83 mil	45.9	1.4	232	74	30.3	.48	78
Iran	78	29	1.92	48	70	7.3	3.9	284
Turkey	76	29.8	2.07	97	74	12.5	2.6	198
Congo	69	17.4	6.08	30	36	2.7	12.5	33
France	65	40.8	1.98	117	87	31.2	8.09	103
U.K.	63	40.4	1.88	261	80	6.6	1	103
Italy	61	44.7	1.46	203	69	11.9	12.26	100
So Africa	53 mil	26.2	2.43	44	63	12.7	31	??
Colombia	48.9	28	2.33	43	76	8.3	32	244
Spain	47	41.8	1.48	93	78	10.4	.8	144
Argentina	41.8	31.3	2.2	15	93	10.2	5.5	149
Poland	38	39.1	1.39	118	61	1.3	1	210
Canada	35.5	40.3	1.66	4	81	30.8	1.6	118
Venezuela	30.9	27.4	2.43	34	94	10.7	45	174
Australia		23.6	37.3	1.88	3	90	15	1.1	143
Netherlands	18.6	42.1	1.77	405	84	3.9	.9	82
Greece	11 mil	43.2	1.51	84	62	22.5	2.	120
Israel	7.8	30.1	2.91	353	92	7.3	1.8	249
Finland	5.4	42.5	1.85	16	84	29.1	1.6	58

COUNTRY	Deaths	capita	crimes
Argentina	10.5		1.34
Australia	.86	15	1.6
Belgium	2.42	1.6	
Brazil	19.03	.8	25.2
Canada	2.22	30.8	2.52
Costa Rica	6.28		8.5
Denmark	1.28	12	.8
France	3.01	31.2	3.77
Germany	1.24	30.3	6.51
Greece	1.64	22.5	1.7
Hungary	.87	5.5	1.3
Iceland	1.57	30.3	.3
India	,48	4.2	1.76
Israel	1,87	7.3	2.23
Italy	1.28	11.9	2.23
Japan	,06	.6	2.85
Mexico	11.17	15	1.52
Netherlands	.46	3,9	1.42
New Zealand	1.45	22,6	.9
Nicaragua	7.29	7.7	11.3
Norway	1.78	31.3	
Portugal	1.77	8.5	1.2
Quatar	.15	19.2	1.1
Russia	11.6	2.95	
South Africa	21,51	12.7	31.0
South Korea	.06	1.1	1.54
Swaziland	37.16	6.4	33.8
Sweden	1.47	31.6	1.23
Switzerland	3.84	45.7	.6
U. Kingdom	.25	6.52	
U. States	10.30	11.88	
Venezuela	50.90	10.7	

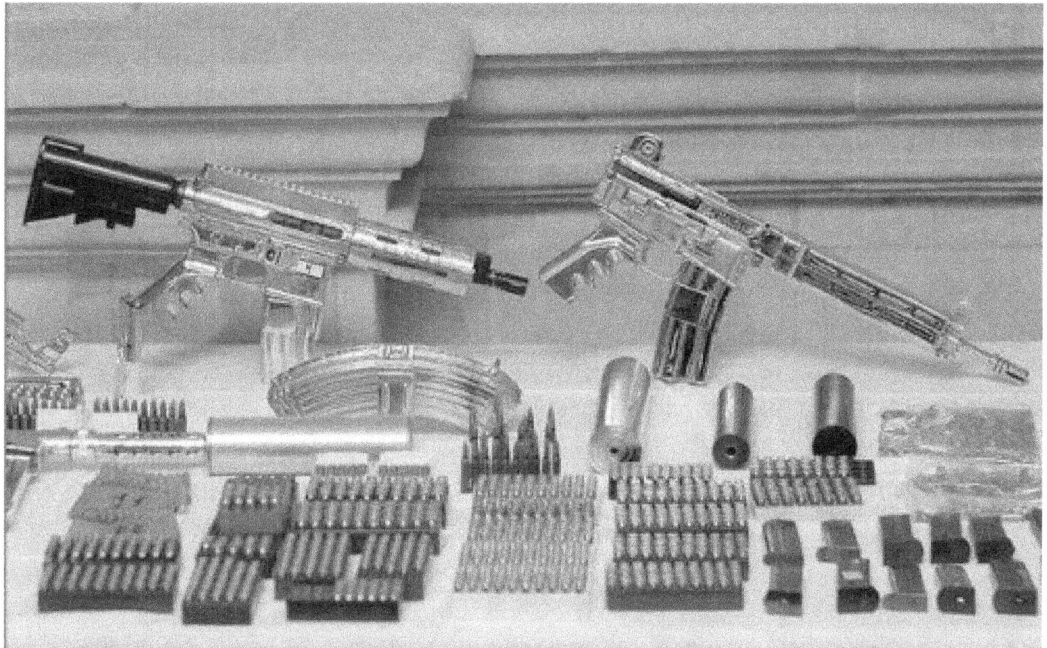

First. IN THE JUNGLE, THE MIGHTY JUNGLE , . . . THE CHARGING ASSAILANT IS ONE HELL OF A LOT MORE BIG AND DANGEROUS . . . . AND OF A VASTLY DIFFERENT SOCIOECONOMIC AND ETHNIC AND RACIAL AND POLITICAL AND RELIGIOUS .. . . EXPERIENCE AND ORIENTATION AND MINDSET . . . . THAN THOSE BEING ATTACKED. (the officials) . . . .

And what is the reaction of the "officials"?

As the enraged, essentially psychopathological creature, totally/terroristically/territorystically intending their murder . . . as it nears . . . .

One of the biologists raises and fires and and the little tranquilizer dart goes plurp into the purp . . . which promptly falls to the ground. When the dna and stool and other samples have been taken, and other official matters completed, the rhino or hippo staggers to its feet and toddles off. Does this not reveal the means to preempt and prevent death by "deadly concerns of circumstances" -- a cop's assessment of his own possible death if he doesn't shoot first?

I picture myself wearing a uniform, alone at the door of a car I've stopped in the night, and I can feel the fear/hate of the four big African men in it and it sure looks like there's something metallic beside the driver and the guy's hand next to him sure looks like it's reaching toward . . . . . .

Would a rational reaction of restraint on my part be to query, "Pardon, sir, but would you please tell me what it is you seem to be intent on taking in hand lest I assume personal vulnerability and perhaps over-react to secure my own sense of safety??"

Could it be that unless you or I or any of us were where cops so often are, we'd really have no "informed, experiential" justification in screaming "police brutality" overall? Though undeniably there are brutal cops and just plain carnage committed. Yes, some cops are deadly animals. It's residual in some humans' nature.

Some of nature's humans.

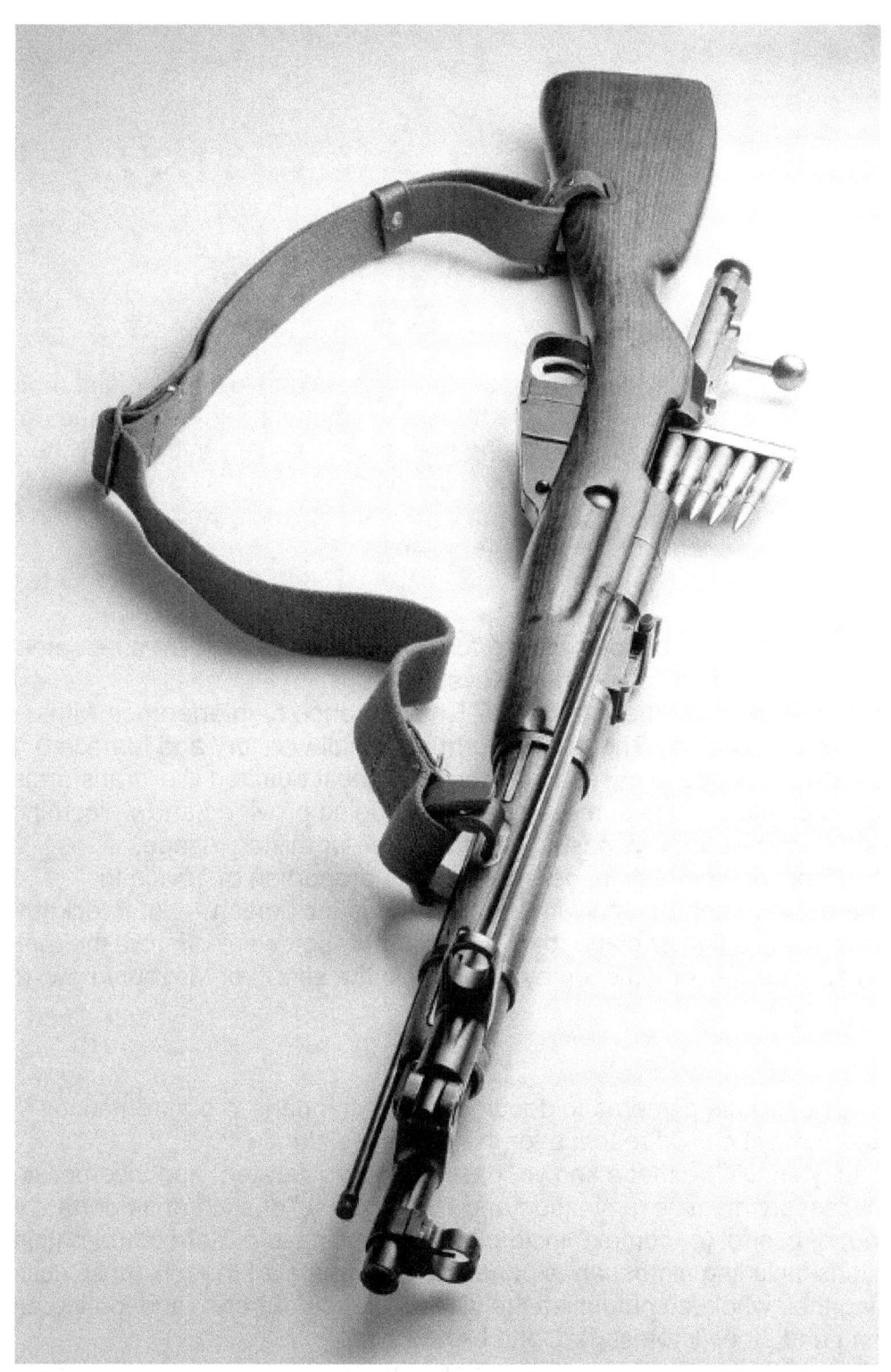

ADDITIONAL ESSAYS AND BLOGS

There's surveillance all over the place: lobbies, parking lots, more and more streets and intersections. Of course there should be cameras recording potential life-and-death confrontations involving the police -- usually initiated by the police in contexts and situations not involving life-or-death at all (such as jay walking or selling cigarettes -- what if it had been by a white guy scalping Met tickets outside Carnegie . . . or Mets outside some stadium?)

As for cop-cams, no, not demeaning to officers even though I'm sure someone other than I would be calling them Keystone cops.
What's the reason for the resistance? Encumbrance or interference with movement or comfort? Those in uniform in the full-war fury and furnace of the Middle East manage in cases when they're almost outfitted like "transformers". As Jared points out, the domestic police are being provided and welcoming (even tanks!!) heavy weaponry "past expiration date" for military usage.
Such will provide protection, deterrence. The proportion of device to demographic (other than a Watts-size venue) is a bit much -- but if rocket launchers and a fighter plane for this or that borough were offered, the materiel would sure be welcomed even by whoever is the sheriff of Maybury now. (or was it Mayberry?)

So why not simple cameras to document what happens in confrontations??
Yet there may be valid reasons for the police resistance.
If so, they should be made known, passed on, proliferated, and incorporated into the necessary media examination and even expose' of such an important issue. For out of control (or context) incidents are resulting in out-of-control nationwide reactions including almost an exponential detrimental of the folk most victimized making their whole communities the victims of their outrage (and looting and burning and other "protests"). Gotta be stopped.
Non-lethal "shoot-to-still" preemption might work. CAMERAS ON COPS MIGHT WORK.
Have I read recently that cameras are being (or have been) installed which record surgeries . . . . . .
Wonder what the reaction of a cop whose kid's going to have a life-threatening operation would be if "surgeons against surveillance cameras" organized?

1 NYC cop dead in shooting, 2nd critical
Note, the following not in perfect time-sequencing.
Very considerate of the shooter to save the City of New York all kinds of legal expenses for prosecution.
Think back, though. This country has always been violent. New York gangs, Chicago, Olde South lynchings, wild West where the cops gunned down were in four-legged cruisers (one man per). The history of New City is actually horrific (incidences of burnings alive, breaking on a wheel, gang wars ("Gangs of New York" the book and movie) Chicago Prohibition era, race riots and industrial uprisings. Essential genocide of the original occupants of our "imminent domain by Manifest Destiny". How recently Watts, the post Rodney King little fracas, Boston as bomb defused perhaps only by Little Richard's calming influence at the old Boston Garden. How about the era of Jewish Communists and Italian anarchists? We are living in a lull, actually. KKK passe'. Just disorganized militias now.
The mass is not -acre or murder. It's media coverage that's a magnifying class of comprehension. For it ain't as bad as it seems 'cept in certain places.

There was a time beginning back in the Bible's beatific reportage when everything was being slaughtered including, intermittently, the slaughterers, when God got perturbed that they weren't being (compensatorily) subservient unto His all-lovingness and he struck down his own chosen people with serpent bites and plagues and pestilences . . . . and each other.
The Greek wars. Trojans. And the rest of the restive residents of the region. Then the less than peaceful Roman empire, Somewhere within the time-span area Hannibal with his elephants for alpine traverse (care to psychoanalyze his fixation perhaps on trunks as phallic symbols by which he could be a conquering man of anything?).

And shifting our coverage to the North, the Vikings and the Scottish and Celtic and Irish against each other and then England into the tag-team terminations of the thousands. And then, somewhat a disrespect of Jesus's sacrifice so that man could live ever in peace and God's grace and even the lion lie down with the lamb (easiest way for the former to dine on the latter). . . . . then (we're skipping back) the era of the early Christian heresies to take some of the load of persecution and torture off the overworked Romans who were losing it in the overinflation of their empire . . . . and then again forward in time and upward in latitude the Catholics v. Protestants and vice versa and Vatican v. Templars who were defiant to the end, singing "come on baby, light my fire." Later, "War of the Roses", "Thirty Years' War" and the entre'acts of axes wielded, and spears and boiling oil.

And, oh yes, a minor matter easy to forget amidst the all these pieces of the pie of peace, the Crusades and Inquisition. And for a time every subdivision of every European's knights and even peasants besieging and slaughtering each other amid breach of wall and brutalizing of woman.
Backflash to Cossacks and Genghises and pan the camera East where China and Japan were kaleidoscopic chaos committed by Shoguns and Samurai (the latter a bit confused, for it's either supposed to be the belly for navel gazing or for gelatinous laughter -- not for slitting (*seppuku,* I think).
And to bring us up to the recent from the distant past, we have the Revolutionary, French and Indian, Civil, Mexican, and ratings wars (where were they fought?) right here on our own field of frenzy.
WW I and II weren't quite intermissions before the short runs of Korea and 'Nam.

A kid here, guy there, a couple by sniper, little group by "shooter" in the theater, and now a couple cops. A tragedy of personal perspective, even mine for I am literally saddened to eye moisture somewhat in telepathic synchrony with what those grieving feel. And the same "vicarious emotion" I've felt to so the parents of or lover or child or spouse . . . . so damned many that one may share the sear of loss, but there isn't enough left to cry with.

Snuff happens. In so many ways.
But less now than through history's misery, man's inhumanity as mystery. Perhaps we need to look at retrospect's panorama, diorama, die-orama and follow time's trajectory as the endless carnage calmed. Why? How? Surely not some random mutation of the complexes and complicities and accomplices of mankind's vestigial predatory programming. If not transcendence as design of spontaneous intelligence to not commit mutual massacre, ... then what hath brought on the periods of peace?
Can we make "peace products"? Surely the people of the world would buy. Coexistence fast food? What a market for servings of serenity.
Or saturation bombing of the warring regions with . . . pornography? What a "diversion tactic".

But seriously, to conclude. Violence unto mindless murder is part of man's mentality.
But through recorded time there's been so much more than now. And without "conventions" and protocols to at least try to control the "excruciating creativity of" the carnage.

Guns in the wrong hands result in tragedy.
Sometimes the wrong hands are those of "law enforcement" personnel.
There may be situations where a cop's preemptive "shoot to kill" prevents his (or another) being killed.
Such was not the situation in Ferguson from all the evidence apparent.
(Do we here have an example of why surveillance cameras have more potential value as evidence -- than privacy-invasive detriment ?)
Frenzied, frightened, momentarily irrational. a cop shooting an assumed assailant might be understood. Once.
There is no understanding multiple shots at a psychological threat!!! An unarmed one. Even if he's a big one.
There are so many locales of the body to which a shot could effectively stop even actual attack in its tracks.
Have we reached a point that the fallacy of generic "gun control" should be inclusive of cops (and the military)?

(Consider -- the extent of governmental regulation of those realms and their qualifications to use weapons).

As I suggested months ago re. "gun control" (partially satirically, PARTIALLY SATIRICALLY, . . . but also with an undercurrent suggestion that my suggestion be taken seriously . . . .

Should the police be armed with tranquilizer guns, their "dart-ammunition" specially calibrated for non-lethal but instant-acting human dosage?? Thus, shoot first, sort it out later??
Or should we just let (beyond mere licensed), officially appointed gun-bearers turn into loose cannons -- killers
. . . . (even if this Ferguson case amounts to a manslaughter, rather than intentioned murder as it seems)

Through the years there have been things that many people have thought would be nice to get rid of. And they've tried to ban card-playing -- theater -- have instated and rescinded prohibition -- they've writhed and rave religiously-emotionally to the writhing and raving of rock and roll performance -- they've conducted a "*defeat* on drugs" for years -- legislated/criminalized prostitution -- and perhaps with a modicum more mentality than regarding other issues . . . . . advocated gun control.

Unless draconian penalties (such as public burning or torture or amputation) would be imposed on violators of forbidden, good luck with the forbidding. And even with horrific consequences for this or that, history reveals that people will still engage in, conduct, commit to, consort with, and even espouse the forbidden even resulting in massacres of which they are significant massacre-ees of the opposing-side who are the massacre-ers.

But there should not be "laissez-faire", legislation-less lenience in perhaps any human behaviors that can have seriously adverse effects on others. This would include activities ranging from "deviant" sexuality (such as sadism) unto international finance (shafting the economic system for the greater erection of the investment industry's mega-shareholders and executives' millions and other bottom-lines (including those comprised of white powder).

No sooner than we should allow a civilian to commute in a Sherman tank should we allow public ownership of assault weapons. Or perhaps the next stage of Gun Lobby lunacy will be to up the ante of amendment guarantee for those who'd want to do target practice with rocket launchers? Even music is subject to some controls such as its volume within contexts or neighborhoods, etc. Card-control might involve some sort of constraint of those who would bankrupt themselves (or finance further fun with crime).

There has to be some control of what otherwise could become chaos. Regarding sexuality, consider some world areas where even child sex ("or you prefer chicken or duck, sir?") is smorgasbord served for the very rich (and in a couple notorious cases clergy). Regarding shooting, consider so many parts of the Middle East).

Child sexual exploitation is a realm apart from examinations of sexual permissions and parameters and premises -- yet depending where even in the US, age of consent in one state would be pedophilia in another. In NY City, late 1800s, the age was 12. In other parts of the world biology is manifestation of consent: puberty. And, of course, through historical eras sexual "adulthood-consent" age has varied vastly. That 18 is "legal" (thus moral? normal?) is a judgmental construct, not a condition of the organism (or orgasmism) of concern. But in this case, 18 (or in a couple other states a couple years younger, I think) should be kept where it's at. (Though we know full well there are myriad "sex-offenders" despite the registry and life-long stigmatization thereof).

And perhaps that's indicative of the gun situation. Enforce whatever prerequisites for ownership, constrain whatever types of the owned, still there will be owners who will be "projectile-perverts" and through the "ways and means" obtain whatever turns them on. And there will be among them the psychos who get it off not just by pulling the trigger, but by offing others -- even children!!!

As for adult sexuality, it could be that our assumption of inherent monogamy, thus matrimony, is perversion. A perspective of nature reveals variety is not only the spread of genetic benefit, but the spice of life. More and more we discover (through DNA) that species once assumed to mate-for-life may associate in "marine or avian marital binary bliss" . . . but fool around on the side too!! Human sexual mores, especially for the "entitled" is blatant evidence that simply one-to-one sexuality "'til death do ye part"" has been not a biological manifestation -- rather a matter of economics. Rich enough, thus the ultra, the elite, you could have hundreds to screw. Yet even the "down-to-earth" of other cultures allow more than one wife. What is a remnant of polygamy in the Middle East is actually a cultural continuum of the Old Testament Jewish laws of "lie-with" lenience (including rather astounding incidences of incest, despite "thou shalt not lie with" declarations).

If controlling guns would control guns I'd be all in favor. That various checks and waiting periods are required for automotive matters or insurance policies etc. exist, surely some equivalent would not be out of line prior to possession and operation of a munitions-vehicle. The point to consider is not, as others have mentioned, that people are killed by cars, yet we don't consider banning cars. For one thing, cars are really necessities. But to the point, if the school or theater or shopping center (or whatever venue) assaults and deaths were being caused by lunatics smashing cars into the premises . . . .
THERE'D SURE AS HELL BE RESTRICTIONS AND REGULATIONS REGARDING WHO COULD DRIVE WHAT IN THE VICINITY.

03/14/2003 to my blogsite

Regarding my 3/9/14 dissertation, it seems I've given a wrong impression, perhaps in part due to the mode of my expression!! "Hyperbole" was a critique term used by a respondee to me. "Terminological terpsichore" (word-dances) is where it's at. Including sometimes compulsive alliteration, I enjoy playing with words. Sometimes "devil's advocate" exaggeration is involved.
Just one example, I phrased "lunatic gun lobby" -- which was an understandable misunderstanding of my intention by a respondent. (But it should be self-evident that the "gun lobby" is not the population of gun-owners!! -- so I was not dissing anyone personally.)

Regarding gun ownership and gun owners, heaven forbid the ignorance, let alone futility, of any attempt to disarm the armed populace of this country. Aside from the Constitutional entitlement and guarantee, basic brain behavior should reveal that in a world of weapons' threats (perhaps so far just latent) abroad -- as well as sporadically domestic . . . . actually being without any means of self-defense may represent group naivite', though maybe not quite stupidity.
Some time or other ago I posted a couple discourses shortly following the Connecticut school shooting. I thought I comprehensively presented a rational analysis of gun issues, including my conclusion that getting trying to get rid of guns would accomplish weapons-worsenings (a la Prohibition).

I'm all in favor of gun ownership. A gun in one's home could very well be equivalent to a "fire-power extinguisher" (should there come an armed intruder . . or eventually insurgent force) . . An actual fire extinguisher to put out actual flames should also be part of one's protection (and I would think required, if not by law, by insurance companies!!!!)
I feel that the gun lobby can be faulted for its abject resistance to registering gun owners, & to some format of background check prior to passing the pistol or other over the counter. Think of the myriad situations (driver's license, insurance, hospital volunteer positions . . . .) that require background screening of the applicant's suitability for whatever. The "Gun Lobby Ludicry" may be that , given its unquestionable influence/clout, it doesn't "legitimize" (even "elevate") its demographic and legislative stance by establishing its own criteria. Thus gun-owners would become an "echelon of the qualified!!!"

I've never owned a gun. But if I were appraised that within X period of time the opportunity for one to purchase a weapon would end, but ownership would be "grandfathered", I'd hasten out to procure one!!!
That's as simply as I can state my position on ownership per se. For me 'twould be a pistol.

Regarding types of weapon . . . another of my issues taken issue with . . . I should think the gun lobby itself would back bans on the ballistic baddies . . . military-style assault weapons -- unless, by specific licensing, for specific "extreme-target" competitions (for example). What rationale, what justification for legal 100-round/seconds (+/-) firepower of a rifle when there's no outcry of threatened autonomy or 2nd Amend. "confiscation" concerning someone owning a bazooka or grenade?

As far as there being "bumps in the road" to impede what I've written previously, I thought I'd leveled the length and breadth of the lanes we travel. Criminalizing whatever, adds criminality to such other concerns (so often subjective) as ethics or morality, kind of synergizing "sin" -- and locking it up in contexts and confines such that the penal system may be the worse crime committed!!

Heaven forbid Sharia -- or Puritan "purity" and punishments -- though such cruelty might equal control.
But some regulation, registration, seems necessary to assure the Constitutional right of the "pursuit of self-preservation" of all Americans.
Or should we do away with all testing and licensing because that might lead to the government taking away our motorcycles . . . . ?

Below, a reader's response to my above 2 postings on Democratichub.com

alongcameaschneider **Wrote:** Regarding my 3/9/14 dissertation, it seems I've given a wrong impression, perhaps in part due to the mode of my expression!! "Hyperbole" was a critique term used by a respondee to me. "Terminological terpsichore" (word-dances) is where it's at. Including sometimes compulsive alliteration, I enjoy playing with words.
Well, you are dancing on a razor-thin line and being I'm the only person that bothered to respond to your March 9th "dissertation", I can say with certainty that you spend most of your time over that line. In all honesty, you should restrict the majority of your writing to just plain English, especially when attempting to write persuasive commentary in which you offer characterizations of people, . . . because your "play with words" alienates people.
    alongcameaschneider **Wrote:** Sometimes "devil's advocate" exaggeration is involved. Just one example, I phrased "lunatic gun lobby" -- which was an understandable misunderstanding of my intention by a respondent. (But it should be self-evident that the "gun lobby" is not the population of gun-owners!! -- so I was not dissing anyone personally.)
And there you expose your profound tone-deafness. The separation of "the gun lobby" and "gun owners" only exists in the minds of anti-gun rights activists. I understand "divide and conquer" is a time tested tactic but it is only effective when a wedge that already exists can be hammered further down.

Let me be perfectly clear; I do take it personally when people denigrate, ridicule and MISREPRESENT the NRA or other organizations that defend rights. You attack them, you attack me.

alongcameaschneider Wrote: Regarding gun ownership and gun owners, heaven forbid the ignorance, let alone futility, of any
attempt to disarm the armed populace of this country. Aside from the Constitutional entitlement and guarantee,
I don't know of anyone on the gun rights side who is 'fearful' of citizen disarmament who thinks that it would be attempted in one fell swoop. It can happen and it is being advocated for, not pressing for "one law does it all", but as a death of a thousand cuts.

alongcameaschneider Wrote: basic brain behavior should reveal that in a world of weapons' threats (perhaps so far just latent) abroad -- as well as sporadically domestic . . . . actually being without any means of self-defense may represent group naivite', though maybe not quite stupidity.
Well, that has existed in selected areas that enacted gun bans. Washington Dc comes to mind where handguns were banned and operational long guns could not be possessed even within one's home.

alongcameaschneider Wrote: Some time or other ago I posted a couple discourses shortly following the Connecticut school shooting. I thought I comprehensively presented a rational analysis of gun issues, including my conclusion that getting trying to get rid of guns would accomplish weapons-worsenings (a la Prohibition).
Well, it doesn't seem that Conneticuit followed your suggestion.

alongcameaschneider Wrote: I feel that the gun lobby can be faulted for its abject resistance to registering gun owners,
And you really think it is just the "the gun lobby" that opposes registration?

PEOPLE resist registration, look what's happening in Connecticut right now! The state bans new "assault weapons" and extended mags, grandfathering those guns and mags already owned. The owners of those grandfathered guns and mags were required to register them and the registration window has closed with only a very small percentage (< 15% ?) of owners complying.

What to do now? As many as 100,000 CT citizens are giving the middle finger to the state, facing being charged with a Class D felony exposing themselves to a maximum sentence of five years in prison and a $5,000 fine . . . and they own 300,000+ of these guns (and a million or more of the other kinds).

Of course some (who won't be responsible for actually walking through the doors) are advocating using the original purchase information (ATF form 4473) to issue warrants and arrest these people - so my side question is, if you already know who owns what, what do you need a registration for ;
). http://articles.courant.com/2014-02-10/business/hc-haar-gun-registration-

[felons...]

Cops and Sheriffs are not too enthusiastic to go busting down the doors of these people, especially enforcing a law that many citizens and many in law enforcement believe is unconstitutional and thus void on its face.

> **alongcameaschneider Wrote:** & to some format of background check prior to passing the pistol or other over the counter. Think of the myriad situations (driver's license, insurance, hospital volunteer positions . . . .) that require background screening of the applicant's suitability for whatever.

Funny that you think that something that happened 21 million times last year, doesn't happen. http://www.fbi.gov/about-us/cjis/nics/reports/1998_2014_monthly_yearly_totals-0... (19KB pdf)

> **alongcameaschneider Wrote:** The "Gun Lobby Ludicry" may be that , given its unquestionable influence/clout, it doesn't "legitimize" (even "elevate") its demographic and legislative stance by establishing its own criteria. Thus gun-owners would become an "echelon of the qualified!!!"

Are you aware that NRA qualification courses are the gold standard for citizen and law-enforcement? Tens of thousands of cops and Sheriffs have trained and qualified under NRA programs supervised by NRA certified range officers. NRA is the "echelon of the qualified" and their commitment to citizen and law enforcement training is ongoing; NRA trains those who train law enforcement. http://le.nra.org/training/instructor-development-schools.aspx

> **alongcameaschneider Wrote:** I've never owned a gun. But if I were appraised that within X period of time the opportunity for one to purchase a weapon would end, but ownership would be "grandfathered", I'd hasten out to procure one!!! That's as simply as I can state my position on ownership per se. For me 'twould be a pistol.

Well, if you do the first thing you should do is sign up for a training / safety course. After graduating you can nail the shingle on your wall and proudly display the NRA logo on your certification. http://goo.gl/xtkg95

> **alongcameaschneider Wrote:** Regarding types of weapon . . . another of my issues taken issue with . . . I should think the gun lobby itself would back bans on the ballastic baddies . . . military-style assault weapons -- unless, by specific licensing, for specific "extreme-target" competitions (for example).

Talk about projecting one's feelings onto others . . .

> **alongcameaschneider Wrote:** What rationale, what justification for legal 100-round/seconds (+/-) firepower of a rifle when there's no outcry of threatened autonomy or 2nd Amend. "confiscation" threat concerning someone owning a bazooka or grenade?

If there is one type of weapon that meets all the criteria of 2nd Amendment protection, it is the type of gun commonly known as an "assault weapon".

> **alongcameaschneider Wrote:** As far as there being "bumps in the road" to impede what I've written previously, I thought I'd leveled the length and breadth of the lanes we travel. Criminalizing whatever, adds criminality to such other

concerns (so often subjective) as ethics or morality, kind of synergizing "sin" -- and locking it up in contexts and confines such that the penal system may be the worse crime committed!!
I haven't a clue what that gibberish means. The speed bumps I was referring to, are the constitutional prohibitions that will knock the wheels off the cart carrying the laws you are pushing (i.e., banning assault weapons).

alongcameaschneider **Wrote:** Heaven forbid Sharia -- or Puritan "purity" and punishments -- though such cruelty might equal control. But some regulation, registration, seems necessary to assure the Constitutional right of the "pursuit of self-preservation" of all Americans.
There is no right, constitutional or otherwise, to be safe or to feel safe. The path of "assuring" a right is not by regulating it. The simple assigning of the term "right" removes that interest from the eyes of government.

Guns Feinstein   (this is worth repeating)

regarding the proposed weapon registration bill and response thereto
(by A. H. Schneider)

Please understand that I thank and admire Cpl Joshua for his
service as a Marine. And I respect the sincerity and recognize
the emotional validity of his response to the proposed gun bill.
And please allow my contrasting, even in points conflicting, response to him.

Joshua seems proud to have served his country as a Marine.
Considering his relation to his country otherwise, his distrust and
> disrespect for his country represents sedition. Such a stance with
> regard to some order or regulation in the Corps would have been
> a punishable offence, possibly unto court marshal.

The President of the United States is the Commander-in chief of the Military.
> The government of the United States is his "chain of command" so to speak. Laws
> are passed by the government within context and constituent ranks
> of the President (so to speak).
>> Cpl. Joshua is blatantly stating his refusal to obey his commander in
>> chief!!

*"I will not register my weapons should this bill be passed, as I do not
believe it is the government's right to know what I own. Nor do I think
it prudent to tell you what I own so that it may be taken from me by a
group of people who enjoy armed protection yet decry me the same
a crime."*

> As a citizen of this country, all the more as a member of the Marine Corp
> or other

armed services of this country, it is not one's singular right to supervene, by evasion
or rebellion or insurrection, the consensus/legislated rules and laws of governance of
this country.
There is not a proposal to confiscate anyone's legally owned weapons.
There is a need to control just who can own what kind of weapon -- or
> would it be the *"you, ma'am have overstepped a line that is not
> your domain. I am a Marine Corps Veteran of 8 years, and I will
> not have some woman who proclaims the evil of an inanimate
> object, yet carries one, tell me I may not have . . . ."* a bazooka,
> a Sherman tank, a live hand grenade, a machine gun, a nuke!!!

*"I am not your subject. I am the man who keeps you free. I am not your
servant. I am the person you serve. I am not your peasant."* What
possible relation does this have to a proposal for some kind of control

over who possesses what devices (guns) that have no other purpose of design or use than collection, target practice, crime, or killing??
In registering an automobile does one act as a "<u>servant</u>"?
In filling out forms and providing information for everything from insurance to internet to bank account is one a "<u>peasant</u>"?

"I am not your servant. I am the person <u>you serve</u>." ??????

No one has proposed taking away anyone's guns.
The idea is to have at least a little control over who gets what kind of guns.

Cpl. Joshua, what if one of those kids in that theater or the Connecticut school had been your son or daughter?? Or, in order not to seem insecure almost unto paranoia, and hypocritical as well . . . . perhaps you should proclaim your rights of refusal to register to vote or drive or bank or go online and you'd better stop paying taxes for all these categories resulting from regulations actually **require that you give up something (such as fees, charges, taxes).**

Registering your semi-automatic probably would require only your signature.
You are the man who fought for your country?
Why then are you fighting against it now?
You are an American? Yet you're telling America that your private/personal premise takes priority?
. . . . . .even when the protection of your fellow-Americans is involved?
You are a Marine. You served your country. It didn't serve you -- except chow.

"I will not be disarmed to suit the fear that has been established by the media and your misinformation campaign against the American people." The fear was established by lunatics with semiautomatic weapons, not the media. That insufficient control of gun purchase exists to keep such massacre-tragedies from happening . . . is this "misinformation".

"**. . . . .against the American people . . .**" The campaign here is Joshua's.
Read his "the pending Feinstein gun bill . . . and a response . . ." piece carefully, analytically.
It used to be . . .my country, right or wrong . . . .
but we've come down to the primacy-priority:
. . . . .MY GUNS RIGHT OR WRONG . . . .

        GUNS ah yes
       (this off the Internet – and wall)
      Ah yes.   (some Congressional? Group had gathered to condemn a shooting, which one I don't know. In the chamber, the father of one of the victims addressed them as follows . . "

"Much of the blame lies here in this room. Much of the blame lies behind the pointing fingers of the accusers themselves."
    . . . .and a poem . . . . which propounds the preposterous premise
    such as some connection between the *"outlawed simple prayer"* and
       "now gunshots fill our classrooms." . . . . and that *"God is what we need".*
His point being that discontinuing school prayer etc. was the cause of the shooting, and those who have passed the laws of the land are thus responsible. Guess that means that the Founding Fathers (separation of church and state) are responsible for school shootings.

    In the actuality of the history of man, in the name of God, not only has the greater frequency and dimension and heinous cruelty of carnage taken place, but, depending on the sectarian standpoint, it was all (not just justified) but sanctified -- "God's will".
This included, way back, killing every man, woman, child, and beast of the of hose already there, now the   "enemy" whose land was

thence occupied . . . in the name of God. And in more recent past, early Christians of one persuasion mutilated and massacred those of another (the heretics) . . . to fill in the blanks between the persecutions by the Romans.

And then came the Catholics vs. Protestants for a couple centuries of Europe's   history -- so god-filled and peaceful????

Then the "will of God" (Manifest Destiny) which sanctified the genocide of a continent's occupants (except for the few survivors "en   Res."

Removing guns is impossible.

Regulating guns **is** possible -- as a partial preventative of guns in the hands of lunatics.

Refusing this is where the NRA is blame-worthy. And a final thought -- with ready access to even assault semi-automatics, it could be that the more "God" is
brought into the equation, the more likely the psychotic would be motivated to commit carnage . . .
in the name of (or delusion of being) . . . .

GOD. . . . .

Gun Ft. Hood

Regarding the massacre at Fort Hood a couple months ago
   The perpetrator's pay continues, but victims of the carnage are not
      sufficiently covered by the military's benefits

     Definitely a despicable situation -- that the "workplace" protections (benefits) provided for those who serve their country, their encompassing "job" description being that they may be sent to die in battle, -- aren't provided comprehensive (more than adequate) monetary as well as medical coverage. That their deaths took place in non-combat, but in-service status, should entitle them to full benefits. Medals of . . .
     . I think

should be awarded as well. But there are protocols and procedures and paradigms of what, who, how.

Definitionally, so to speak, the "workplace violence" rather than "combat" categorization has background basis. It's a legal (here, military domain) situation. As in whatever prior on-base crimes, the present massacre cannot be extra-legally prosecuted just on 1) the basis of the horrific severity -- or 2) on the ethnicity or religion of the perpetrator. The terms "Jihad" and "terrorist" are so comforting to apply, but within the American context of justice and the apparent details of the shootings, those even *self-assumed roles of the criminal* do not establish the systemic actualities otherwise.

The same situation and outcome, perpetrated by almost anyone of any other persuasion, would not warrant a proliferated contextualization -- such as this case. Here we have a psychopathic mass-murderer. That he's collecting pay the while he's incarcerated waiting trial . . . . 1) I'd imagine that pay's being "held in some kind of 'escrow'." He ain't getting his checks or chits. 2) If convicted, that pay will be, so to speak, retro-actively forfeited . . . . or 3) if not, lawyers have families that need groceries and gas . . . . . .

Moussawi (was that the fool who only wanted to learn how to fly aloft, not take-off or land?) . . . his intention (as one of the 9/11-15) was to create far more carnage than this shooter. Granted, from one spectrum-perspective, he didn't actually do it . . . . but from the apposite end of consideration, he was processed through our civilian legal system, sentenced, and now wanes away for probably the rest of his life in the solitary silence of Pelican Bay.

I believe we should so process this despicable human. By OUR humane processes of administrating justice. Based on our legal system: sometimes fallacious, but overall meticulous legal intricacies, definitions, contextualizations.

The inhumane protection of our service personnel in any situation, especially such as mass-murder and mutilation, is a separate matter. The military should be brought to trial for such dereliction of duty.

By Catherine Cloutier Globe Staff April 20, 2015

The number of "license to carry" gun permits issued in Massachusetts spiked last year in anticipation of last summer's passage of a sweeping gun control bill that tightened the state's already strict firearms laws, according to a Globe analysis of state firearms data.

In the months prior to the law's signing, many gun owners feared firearm licenses would soon be restricted or even eliminated, so "people wanted to make sure they got the license in case the state did something to limit them," said Wayne Sampson, executive director of the Massachusetts Chiefs of Police Association. "There was a huge uptick while the Legislature was debating this issue," he said.

Statewide, the number of active Class A licenses the so-called license to carry category that broadly includes the right to carry a concealed weapon grew nearly 12 percent between 2013 and 2014. That was a significantly greater jump than in past years, a Globe review of data from the Firearms Records Bureau found.

Overall, the number of active gun licenses of all types grew 5 percent, with a total of 355,272 in the state last year.

All but five of Massachusetts' 351 towns and cities saw increases in the number of active Class A licenses from 2013 and to 2014.

The new legislation, which passed in August, built on the state's 1998 gun laws, often considered the toughest in the country.

Among the provisions included in the law was tightening the requirements for applicants seeking the state's Firearm Identification Card to match those of the Class A license perhaps most notably, adding a provision that allows police chiefs to petition the courts to deny a Firearm Identification Card to an applicant not judged suitable. The Firearm Identification Card lets holders possess and transport a rifle or shotgun.

The change was opposed by the National Rifle Association, which said on its website that giving police chiefs such discretion could allow licensing officials to deny Firearm Identification Card applicants on "mere arrests or police contacts that never led to judgments by a court." NRA officials did not return multiple Globe requests for comment.

The new law did not change the basic requirements to get a Class A license. Applicants must still pass a background check and get approval from their community's licensor, often the chief of police. New applicants must also provide proof of firearm safety training. Even then, firearm licenses need to be renewed every six years.

"When you get a license, you have a card saying you're a law-abiding citizen," said Leo Richards, 51, of Framingham, a firearm safety instructor and partner at the Weston Shooters Club.

The legislation did streamline the license renewal process, and required a written justification for license denials.

"There was a lot of concern on the part of the firearm-owning community" about the legislation, said state Representative Harold Naughton, a Democrat from Clinton who chairs the Joint Committee on Public Safety and Homeland Security. "But we said all along our goal was to produce balanced legislation."

With about 318,000 licensees in 2014, the Class A license was the most popular in the state; only about 34,000 residents held Firearm Identification Cards.

Following passage of the new law, more gun license applicants, including former Firearm Identification Card holders, are opting for the higher-level permit, said Sampson. And the Gun Owners' Action League now encourages its members and trainees to get the Class A license, said Jim Wallace, the league's executive director.

Jason Gregg, 39, said he upgraded his lapsed Firearm Identification Card to a Class A license following the change.

"It's $100 for the Firearm Identification Card and $100 for the license to carry. It's the same application, just a different box," said Gregg, who lives in Framingham.

Last year's spike in Class A licenses followed lesser annual increases with a median of 5 percent over the past several years. Since 2008, the number of these licenses has grown in all but two Massachusetts municipalities, Gosnold and Chesterfield. In 11 communities, including Boston, the number has more than doubled.

An immodest proposal (a very variagated variation on Swift's "modest proposal" re. the Irish famine)

Total nudity as crowd security.
At any public event, everyone, participants and observers, should be totally undressed.
Those arriving by public transit would have disrobed at the various stations where they boarded.
Those arriving by their autos would strip before exiting the parking lots.
Those coming on foot from proximate locations would have left their clothes back in their apartments or condos
Everyone approaching the event, indoor or outdoor, would be naked. Totally. No way to carry or wear anything explosive (or otherwise) if you are only clad in your skin (and this might mean that exceptionally hairy people would be banned -- or scanned . .
But explosives come in various forms and configurations, some of which could easily be "internalized" (to put it politely). Thus . . . everyone would have to pass through scanning devices as they approached the locale of the event.
Obviously this sort of super-security system offers at least three advantages:
Far fewer people would attend anything if they had to go naked. This would especially apply to those of Islamic beliefs
Participants in demanding physical activities would be more comfortable wearing less, and might even feel more "classical" (in that original Olympics were done naked)
Events would be held when in warm places or temperatures.
And finally, people might start paying more attention to the condition of their bodies!!!

DISARMING THE POPULACE

There might be a way.
It might be a bit extreme.
But there's precedent for this kind of extreme.
Elsewhere even now.
Criminals (such as thieves) are punished by amputations.
Why not here?
Why not just criminalize gun possession.
No need to take the fire arms away.
Take the arms away – of those who are found to possess the criminal entity – the gun – any kind.

With current technology, some kind of sensor-surveillance would lock onto the location of a gun. The Gun-gone Enforcement guys would obtain warrants. There'd be no illegal search. There'd be appropriate process for them to enter the residence, apartment, loft, co-op, hovel, culvert . . . . wherever a gun has been techno-located. And the residents thereof, anywhereof, would be taken into custody.

If a family, after putting the fear of God or Allah or Buddha or Krishna or whomever into the women and older children, they would be given refreshments and then a ride back to their premises.
A first time capture individual (loner) or head of household would be subjected to 40 lashes, but if having willingly surrendered his firearm (s) prior to the punishment, and evidencing regret for his not having willingly turned the items in before, he would be released.
A second offense would bring all concerned (one if just an individual, the whole family if that applied) to the public square.
> The populace would be required to attend the affair, those employed dismissed from work for the brief period. Thus as a public punishment, the two-timer would have his arms cut off. For 2nd offense possession of a small hand gun, below the elbows would allow some jury-rig prosthetic to be home-made so he could at least perform some functions of self-sufficiency such as wiping.

For 2nd time possession of a high caliber device, the arms would be amputated just below the shoulders. (For even first discovery of concealed assault-type weapon, the "short-sleeves" cut-offs would be the punishment.

But notwithstanding such Draconian barbarity (as gun-control extreme), there would be those (males) who would still hang onto and hide their guns, defying any legislation or amputation threat. Some might wrap the gun in foil or even create a concealing "capsule" impervious to the tech sensor – perhaps using a roll of lead roof flashing. This would work for only awhile before the tech would be able to probe any substance and recognize a concealed weapon.

Such concealment, or any third-time apprehension of a weapon not having been promptly and voluntarily donated to the Department of Collections would result in another public spectacle, family members given front row seats, the populace surrounding the platform where the castration would take place.

One might assume that this paradigm would result in no more fire arms and a lot less appendage arms and after the first or second castration, a decrease of that device of hardly more than 2 or 3 from the whole male population, the rest of whom would rush to pre-emptively get rid of their guns rather than their genitals. But no doubt that wouldn't be the case.
There'd be those who'd give up anything other than their guns.

The next stage after castration would be, for a subsequent gun possession, to watch wife and kids decapitated.
But gun possession isn't so easily surrendered, betrayed, as a man's ultimate entitlement.
    A man's essential self-assertion and recognition of what's of value in life.

"Ya can take all kinds of shit from me, but you'll never get me to just give up what really makes me a man."

    No, even by disarming, even by dismembering, there'll never be the total disarming of the public.

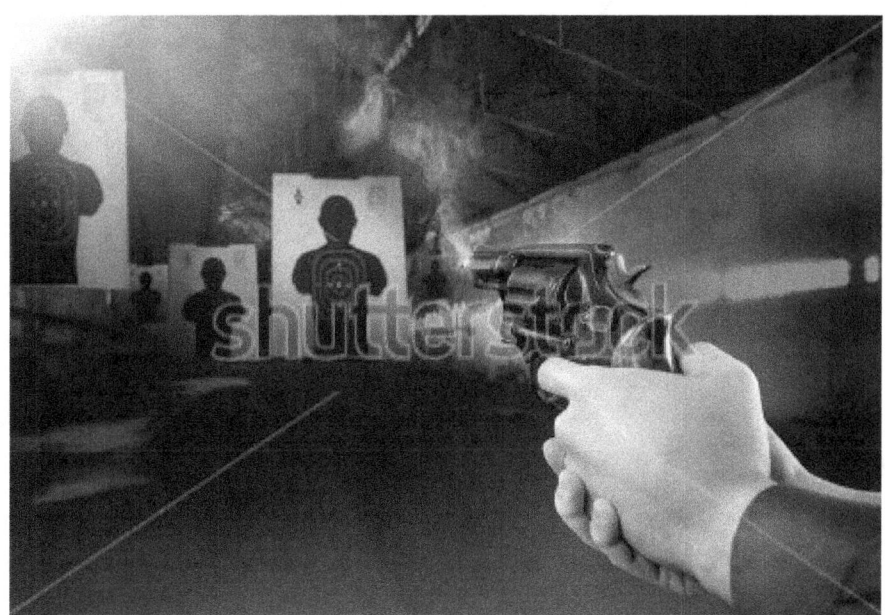